WATCHING OVER ONE ANOTHER IN LOVE

RECLAIMING THE WESLEYAN RULE OF LIFE FOR THE CHURCH'S MISSION

*A Spiritual Formation Resource for
United Methodists & Other Heirs of the Wesleyan Tradition*

Michael G. Cartwright with Andrew D. Kinsey

WIPF & STOCK · Eugene, Oregon

WATCHING OVER ONE ANOTHER IN LOVE
Reclaiming the Wesleyan Rule of Life for the Church

Copyright © 2011 Michael G. Cartwright and Andrew D. Kinsey. All rights reserved. Except for brief quotations in critical publications or reviews, no part of this book may be reproduced in any manner without prior written permission from the publisher. Write: Permissions, Wipf and Stock Publishers, 199 W. 8th Ave., Eugene, OR 97401.

Wipf & Stock
An imprint of Wipf and Stock Publishers
199 W. 8th Avenue, Suite 3
Eugene OR, 97401
www.wipfandstock.com

ISBN 13: 978-1-61097-533-9

The John Wesley monogram on cover and on selected pages throughout the booklet are used by permission of the United Methodist Publishing House, publisher of The United Methodist Hymnal *(1989).*

Manufactured in the U.S.A.

TABLE OF CONTENTS

A Prayer for the Church in Mission 4

Foreword by Andrew D. Kinsey 5

Praising God with John and Charles Wesley 7

Introducing the Wesleyan Rule of Life 8

A Note for Readers of the Daily Reflections 11

Praising God with John and Charles Wesley 13

Week One

    Prayer 15

    Daily Reflections 16

    Praising God with John and Charles Wesley 23

Week Two

    Prayer 25

    Daily Reflections 23

    Praising God with John and Charles Wesley 33

Week Three

    Prayer 35

    Daily Reflections 36

    Praising God with John and Charles Wesley 43

Week Four

    Prayer 45

    Daily Reflections 46

    Praising God with John and Charles Wesley 53

Afterword by Michael G. Cartwright 54

Acknowledgments 59

Appendix A: "The General Rules of the United Societies" (1743) 60

Appendix B: "A Prayer for Those Convicted of Sin" 62

Endnotes 63

A PRAYER FOR THE CHURCH IN MISSION

As we anticipate gathering with other United Methodists and Wesleyan Christians, we give God thanks for the liberty that we have to worship in safety.

We give thanks to the Lord, and we pray that gathering with friends and neighbors for worship and prayer will be a means of grace we will not take for granted.

And so, we pray to God….

We pray that we will remember with gratitude your servants John and Charles Wesley; their parents, Samuel and Susanna; and the rich spiritual heritage that we as 21st-century heirs have received because of their faithful witness.

We give God thanks for works of mercy, for practices of reaching out to the poor, clothing the naked, and visiting the prisoner; we give thanks for how these practices have opened our own eyes to the possibilities for Christian discipleship. For we confess how at times we are distracted by our own wants and needs, and we confess how we need you, Lord, to help us to see those who are in need around us. Forgive us, we pray.

Help us to be alert to the moving of your Holy Spirit and to the power of your grace.

Help us to walk as Jesus walked and to have the mind of Christ.

For we give God thanks and praise for the many "Methodists" who have lived their lives with imaginations that were illumined by your Spirit.

We give you thanks for friendships across the years.

We pray we will continue to strive to be faithful stewards of all you have given us in Christ.

And so, help us, gracious Lord, to be responsive to the needs of those around us.

Help us learn to keep the Sabbath holy and to cultivate the kind of holy imagination that can see the opportunity to do all the good you have called us to do.

In Christ's name, we pray. Amen.

FOREWORD

One of the most important developments in the contemporary renaissance of Christian spiritual practice has been the restoration of the notion of a "rule of life." As Marjorie Thompson explains: *"A rule of life is a pattern for spiritual disciplines that provides structure and growth in holiness. . . . A rule of life . . . is meant to help us establish a rhythm of daily living, a basic order within which new freedoms can grow. A rule of life, like a trellis, curbs our tendency to wander and supports our frail efforts to grow spiritually."* [1]

As contemporary United Methodist pilgrims experiment with the practice of living according to a rule of life, it is possible to *begin drawing new connections* with our own tradition of spirituality.

Although many contemporary United Methodists seem not to realize that this was the case, once upon a time Christian seekers in the Wesleyan tradition had such a pattern for spiritual growth. Although vestiges of what Michael Cartwright prefers to call "the Wesleyan rule of life" can be seen in several different strands of the United Methodist tradition, in almost all cases this pattern comes into focus in the context of living according to the document that is known as "The General Rules of the United Societies" (see Appendix). It was incorporated in the Constitution in 1808.[2]

And for much of the nineteenth century, American Methodists continued to write commentaries on the General Rules. Unfortunately, most of them tended to focus more on the moral issues of the day than on patterns of integrity for Christian spiritual living. As a result, American Methodists began to lose sight of the ways that the General Rules could be used for purposes of spiritual formation.

Over the past two decades, as Michael has led retreats in the Academy for Spiritual Formation (Alabama, Wisconsin, Nebraska, Texas) and the Hinton Colleague Covenant Forum (Indiana, North Carolina, Tennessee) he has became convinced that someone needed to take the first-step in restarting the dialogue in United Methodism about what it means to have a rule of life for spiritual formation. The material presented here is a step in that direction.

What Michael has done is create a resource that can be used by *two groups of people*: clergy and laity. It is a commentary that has been designed as a daily devotion according to a four-week cycle as well as a resource for self-examination for Covenant Groups attempting to "watch over one another in love." Of course, we would hope that all United Methodists who are serious about the Christian life and ministry would be inclined to use this material. But we hope especially that persons who are preparing for ordination as deacons and elders will find this resource to be helpful.

In order to bring the Wesleyan rule of life back into focus, then, Michael has chosen to emphasize the threefold feature of the "General Rules" for each day. This reading of the General Rules affirms that when we take the time to articulate the relationship between the means of grace with the particular affirmations and admonitions of the General Rules, the "rule of life" reemerges. While some readers initially may find this pattern of reflection awkward, Michael's hope is that, as you live with the General Rules in your daily devotions, you will find that a deeper appreciation for the integrity of the Wesleyan "trellis" for spiritual formation will grow.

This project is a joint effort to make the General Rules accessible to a wider audience. As such, readers will notice how Michael and I have divided the daily reflections into four components: (a) the excerpt from the General Rules; (b) a recommended reading from the Bible; (c) a commentary on the rules; and (d) a short devotional prayer. Michael has selected the Rules and written the commentary; I have written the prayers and selected the scripture. The goal has been simply to restore a pattern of reflection from early Methodism and include selected hymns from Charles Wesley.

For the most part, the sequence of daily commentary follows the text of the General Rules as it is presented in the *United Methodist Book of Discipline* since it was fixed by General Conference of 1804. Michael has altered the sequence at a couple of points in order to break up the list of "buying and selling" rules or to correlate the means of grace with particularly apt examples of *"doing no harm, avoiding evil of every kind"* or *"doing good as much as possible."*

But he has tried whenever possible to go with the "sequences" as they fall in the three sections of the document. Those phrases from the original text that are the focus of the daily reflection are in boldface text, with other material from the GR document italicized. Michael also has added introductory lines for each day's reflection on the General Rules to remind us about the covenantal framework within which the particular features of the Wesleyan Rule make sense.

In addition to the six "gospel ordinances" that Wesley listed in the General Rules of the United Societies, Michael has incorporated the practice of giving and receiving counsel or "Christian conference," which simply makes explicit for 21st-century readers what 18th-century readers in early British and American Methodism would have grasped more readily. Readers will notice that the seven means of grace are repeated on the same day of the week for the four weeks. Each commentary begins with the means of grace for the day and works through the positive and negative rules with the particular "gospel ordinance" in view.

To be sure, there are other correlations that can be made with respect to the General Rules. In fact, that is part of the point Michael and I want to make with this commentary: *there are more connections available in the Wesleyan theological tradition than contemporary United Methodists now are exploring.* We would be delighted if other United Methodists would offer such "readings" of the General Rules; they could help us all "connect the dots" as a result of reading and using this resource.

It is not a mere coincidence that Michael began trying to write a commentary on the General Rules after participating in a consultation that brought Methodist and Benedictine leaders together to explore the intersection of these two streams of Christian spirituality. Benedictines regard the *Rule of St. Benedict* as a treasure of Christian wisdom. United Methodists have not always taken the time to engage the General Rules as a piece of wisdom literature. We United Methodists need to make a concerted effort to continue "remembering" the Wesleyan rule of life that Michael and others have begun. It is now time that we United Methodists bring forth our own treasures of Christian wisdom!

As mentioned above, readers will notice how Michael has worked to include selected hymns of Charles Wesley at various points in the text as well as to make particular references to a few hymns in the daily commentaries. This is a connection that many United Methodists have all but lost, as most versions of the General Rules that were published in the eighteenth century included the hymn by Charles Wesley entitled *"A Prayer for Those Who Are Convinced of Sin"* (see Appendix B).

Careful readers will notice how Michael incorporates the Hymn on Gospel Ordinances on the following page and makes connections with hymns at other points.

Michael is keenly aware of the fact that, while he has projected a set of uses for this commentary, readers will discover their own uses. As stated, this commentary may serve also as an aid to personal reflection and examination of conscience, as well as a helpful tool to covenant groups in which "brothers" and "sisters" who have been "united with one another in Christ" are already daring to entrust themselves to one another in humility, believing that God is gifting them to one another at this time in their lives to "watch over one another in love."

—*Andrew D. Kinsey*

PRAISING GOD WITH JOHN & CHARLES WESLEY

"A Hymn on Gospel Ordinances" (*Hymns on the Lord's Supper*, No. 62) is not one of the hymns of Charles Wesley that is well-known to the present generation of United Methodist clergy and laity. However, this poetic text is probably one of the best resources for conveying the directive purpose of the seven Methodist practices associated with the General Rules:

The public worship of God
The ministry of the Word, either read or expounded
The Supper of the Lord
Family and private prayer
Searching the Scriptures
Fasting or abstinence
Giving and receiving counsel or Christian Conference

Like the stars used by navigators to plot the course of ships at sea, these practices enable "serious seekers" to keep their eyes on the prize.

The heavenly ordinances shine,
And speak their origin Divine;
The stars diffuse their golden blaze,
And glitter to their Maker's praise;

They each in different glory bright,
With stronger or with feebler light
Their influence on mortals shed,
And cheer us by their friendly aid.

The gospel ordinances here
As stars in Jesus' church appear;
His power they more or less declare,
But all His heavenly impress bear.

Around our lower orb they burn,
And cheer and bless us in their turn,
Transmit the light by Jesus given,
The faithful witnesses of heaven.

They steer the pilgrim's course aright,
And bounteous of their borrow'd light
Conduct throughout the desert way,
And lead us to eternal day.

We should be grateful that Charles and John Wesley were so adept in providing imaginative resources for the people called Methodists—then and now—to embody believing love and loving obedience. One way to do that is to *use the spiritual inheritance that we have been given* as heirs of the Wesleyan movement as a set of navigational devices for the journey that is ahead.

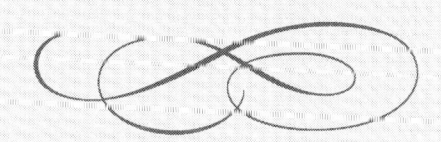

INTRODUCING THE WESLEYAN RULE OF LIFE

"Watching over one another in love" is a winsome phrase that not only is deeply rooted in the Wesleyan tradition but also reminds us that Methodist spirituality is deeply biblical (see Ephesians 4:14-16; Colossians 3:16).

I like to use the three words on the cover of this booklet to explain the Wesleyan rule of life for spiritual formation. *Believe. Love. Obey.* It really can be that simple—provided that we understand that these actions are not to be understood in isolation from one another. I like to think that the dots between these words that surround the JW monogram join them together. The Wesleyan rule of life is about believing love and mutual accountability.

If we are honest with ourselves, we probably need to admit that "watching over one another in love" describes the kinds of relational bonds about which 21st-century United Methodists sometimes feel ambivalent. On the one hand, we long for deeper relationships with people that we respect and trust—within and beyond the congregations in which we are members. On the other hand, we are not sure that we really want to share "how it is with our soul and body"—perhaps because we are afraid of the prospect of rejection and/or disapproval. For that very reason, I have chosen to highlight the ways in which the Wesleyan rule of life operates in a conversational framework that is framed by believing love and mutual obedience.

Simply put, from a Wesleyan perspective, mutual care for one another in the context of a shared covenant is the primary means by which the "trellis" of Christian spiritual formation is constructed and maintained. Accordingly, "The Nature, Design and General Rules of the United Societies" begins with these words:

Such a society is no other that "a company of men 'having the form, and seeking the power of godliness,' united in order to pray together, to receive the word of exhortation, and to watch over one another in love, that they may help each other to work out their salvation."[3]

Christian monasticism is defined by the relationship of spiritual authority that exists between the monk and the abbot as specified in the vows of stability, obedience, and conversion of life. Not surprisingly, the Benedictine "rule of life" unfolds in the context of the kind of spiritual direction that pertains to such vows. In early Methodism, by contrast, while roles were distinguished in various ways (class leaders, preachers, exhorters, etc.), everyone was understood to share the covenant obligations. Among other things, this involved participating in an ongoing conversation with other "brothers" and "sisters" committed to speaking the truth in love.

Practicing Believing Love— Faith Seeking Understanding

The purpose of such conversations, of course, was to explore the faith in a serious way. John Wesley distinguished between the kind of "serious seeking" in which persons were willing to be mentored in the faith and the kind of self-indulgent spiritual quests that do not require self-examination.

He explains his strategy in "The Nature, Design and General Rules" document: "That it may the more easily be discerned whether they are indeed working out their own salvation, each Society is divided into smaller companies, called Classes, according to their respective places of abode. There are about twelve persons in every class, one of whom is styled the Leader."[4]

The fact that the Wesleyan rule of life is organized for the purpose of mentoring should not surprise us. In a very real sense, John Wesley imagined the early Methodist societies as a context for spiritual formation, which included religious instruction or catechesis. The select societies, class meetings, and bands served the diverse needs of men and women who were serious enough to want to explore further. When all of these provisions are viewed together, the Methodist "societies" in England (and later the congregations of American Methodism) were schools for obedience. To use a phrase many Christian traditions recognize, Methodist spirituality begins with "faith seeking understanding." One of the reasons that the Wesleyan "way" of discipleship attracted people was because serious seekers had the opportunity to find answers to questions that they had about the Christian faith as well as to build relationships with persons of spiritual maturity who could provide guidance.

There is only one condition . . . required of those who desire admission into these societies: "a desire to flee from the wrath to come, and to be saved from their sins." But wherever this is really fixed in the soul, it will be shown by its fruits.

It is therefore expected of all who continue therein that they should continue to evidence their desire for salvation, by . . . First, by doing no harm . . . Second, by doing good . . .Third, by attending upon the ordinances.[5]

This sequence displays something quite remarkable. On the one hand, the stated condition for becoming part of these little communities of faith exploration was based on a simple recognition on the part of participants that each person needs to be reconciled with God. Twenty-first-century readers sometimes stumble over the language of "the wrath to come." Early Methodists were very much aware of the prospect of divine judgment and they were well-acquainted with the biblical images (cf. 2 Peter 3:6-15) that imaged the great and terrible Day of the Lord, at which judgment would take place. And the Methodist preachers and class leaders encouraged persons under conviction of sin to remember that the delay in judgment was itself an indication of God's patience, "not wanting any to perish, but all to come to repentance" (2 Peter 3:9b). This kind of active interpretation is appropriate when the purpose of a group of people is to enable one another to find their way back into relationship with the Triune God.

Practicing Loving Obedience— Developing Mutual Accountability

In addition to being given the opportunity to deepen their faith through greater understanding of the Christian life, persons who wanted to continue to be "members" of the Methodist societies, bands, and class meetings were required to *show evidence* of their *ongoing desire for salvation.* They did so by being accountable to one another for their behaviors and intentions with other ordinary Christian people, as well as to subject themselves to ongoing conversation about their progress in moving away from disordered desires toward the kind of holy desires that fostered spiritual growth.

To use a more contemporary image, the kind of community that Wesley is describing might best be described as "an open circle"[6] formed by serious seekers who dare to believe that God has given them to one another for the purpose of spiritual growth. That is to say, the classes, bands, societies, and conferences of preachers were intended to be *ordered communities of hospitality and holiness*[7] in which laymen and laywomen as well as ordained clergy engaged one another in disciplined conversation, daring to speak the truth in love with one another in the hope that God would use their conversations to enable further spiritual growth for all of them. Of course, as anyone who has ever tried to maintain a circle while being receptive to newcomers knows, the figure of an "open circle" is *difficult but not impossible* to maintain.

Anyone who has ever watched a marching band perform knows that such an event does not happen without a lot of practice. When the group begins the year, everyone has to learn to march *together.* And that takes hours and hours of working together. As the parent of four children who have all participated in the local high school's marching band, I am always amazed at what happens between late May (when the group initially forms) and the end of the season (when they are competing with other bands at contests). Some of the geometrical figures that I have seen this company of 14- to 18-year-olds perform on football fields at halftime on fall evenings are simply amazing. And every year they have to *re-form* the band. That is, the band needs to be disciplined enough for everyone to march together but needs to be flexible enough to incorporate new members who join the group at the beginning of each season. With discipline and flexibility, they can perform as an open circle of musicians.

Although I would be the first to say that this analogy is not adequate to convey all the dynamics of the Wesleyan rule of life for spiritual formation, I like to use it because it reminds us of the ways that we do depend on one another to accomplish something greater than what we could do by ourselves. Some band members march better than others. Some tuba players play better than others, and everyone has to depend on the drum majors as well as the drum captain in order to perform their choreographed musical production.

I also like the marching band image as a metaphor for spiritual formation in the Wesleyan tradition because it reminds us that *not all mistakes are equally significant.* I have often been fascinated to learn that band members are more critical of a performance than are those viewing it from the stands, because the band members are more aware of their individual capacities to make mistakes. When viewed as a whole, the various imperfections of a particular performance may or may not turn out to be significant, because much depends on the combined performance. Regardless, every person in the band needs to be committed to doing his or her best in order for the band to succeed. That is mutual accountability.

"Watching over one another in love" requires that we have a realistic awareness of our own strengths and weaknesses as individuals and as a group. John Wesley was pessimistic about what human beings can do apart from God's grace, but he was optimistic about what can happen by the power of the Holy Spirit working in us.

Consider another analogy. Imagine that you and several friends are out for a day of sailing. You are all having a good time together when the wind suddenly dies. At first you are not concerned, because you are still enjoying yourselves. Then you realize that without wind it is going to be very difficult to get back to shore (there is no auxiliary motor available on this boat!). At first you try to paddle along, but your sailboat doesn't move very far. Then you and your friends jump overboard and try to push the boat forward by swimming. Eventually you realize that you are facing the prospect of being stuck out in the middle of the lake. A few hours pass, and then you begin to feel something. A faint breeze is beginning to stir. You and your friends begin to exercise whatever sailing skills you may have to manipulate the sails and position the boat to catch the wind. Thanks to your collective efforts—and the wind!—you are able to tack back and forth and eventually make your way back to shore.

John Wesley treated the commandments of the Sermon on the Mount and other passages of scripture as "covered promises." That is, they were *commands that could be obeyed because God provides the grace* that enables us to fulfill what is required.[8] Thus, we love our enemies in response to Jesus' teaching in the Sermon on the Mount not because we possess superhuman conscience, but rather because God provides us with the grace necessary to do his will in particular circumstances. The practices of giving and receiving counsel and searching the scriptures were intended to be "means of grace" that not only represented skills to be developed but also channels for the guidance of the Holy Spirit. To use the words of Charles Wesley's wonderful hymn, these "gospel ordinances" provided the kind of guidance that makes it possible to "steer the pilgrim's course aright . . ." regardless of whatever "dark night of the soul" he or she might be experiencing at a particular juncture in life.

Continuing the sailing metaphor, it makes sense for more experienced sailors to offer counsel to less-experienced practitioners of the art of sailing so *that all may benefit*. As you rediscover the "Wesleyan rule of life" in the context of using this resource, I hope that you will grow in confidence and realize that, by God's grace and by the Spirit's power and presence, it is possible to live a disciplined life conformed to the image of Christ.

—*Michael Cartwright, Advent, 2010*

A NOTE FOR READERS OF THE DAILY REFLECTIONS

In recent years, United Methodists have been invited to re-engage the General Rules. Reuben Job's book *Three Simple Rules* (Abingdon, 2007) has been read with appreciation by many clergy and laity. And more recently, Kevin Watson has published a book about the General Rules that is aptly titled *A Blueprint for Christian Discipleship: Wesley's General Rules as a Guide for Christian Living* (Discipleship Resources, 2009).

I am grateful that these books are available and I heartily commend them to readers for the purposes for which they were written. Where these resources call attention to the broader directives of this treasure of early Methodism, my own effort is intended to encourage engagement with the canonical text of the General Rules.

I have used three different fonts for the purpose of drawing attention to the threefold aspect of the Wesleyan rule of life in the 28 daily reflections on the General Rules. *Italicized material* is from the original text of the General Rules (see Appendix A). **Boldface text** is used to highlight those phrases that are the focus of a particular day's reflection. Material that has been re-phrased by Michael Cartwright is always presented in a regular font, but where this material is added (as in the case of "giving and receiving counsel or Christian Conference") to be included as a primary focus, such text is also in boldface enclosed with brackets. I have also avoided the use of ellipses except where it provides clarity, and I have altered the case letters where the reshaped text no longer retains the original sentence structure.

Finally, since one of my goals is to encourage United Methodists to engage the original text of the General Rules, I suggest that you read the General Rules *as a whole* once each week during the period that you are using this resource. (Until 1964, it was a rule that at least once a year all Methodist clergy would read the text of the General Rules from the pulpit of the congregations that they served.) That should help you to keep the larger context in view as you read the daily reflections.

And I would hope that the more familiar that we become with the General Rules, the more likely it will be that we will find ways to adapt this text to the challenging circumstances in which we live and serve in the 21st century.

WATCHING OVER ONE ANOTHER IN LOVE

BELIEVE · LOVE · OBEY

PRAISING GOD WITH JOHN & CHARLES WESLEY

"Sinners, Turn, Why Will You Die?" (No. 346 in *The United Methodist Hymnal*) is one of the great "invitation hymns" written by Charles Wesley. Drawing on imagery from the Old Testament prophetic utterances of Ezekiel, the hymn displays the hospitality of the Triune God to each human being as persons created in the image and likeness of God. The first three verses display the persons of the Trinity pleading with the sinner to return to communion with God.

> Sinners, turn; why will you die?
> God, Your Maker, asks you why.
> God, who did your being give,
> made you himself that you might live;
> he the fatal cause demands,
> asks the work of his own hands.
> Why, you thankless creatures, why
> will you cross his love, and die?

Verse five of the hymn indicates the extent of God's mercy, which re-creates God's original intentions for all humankind as depicted in Ezekiel 18:31-32.

> You, whom he ordained to me
> transcripts of the Trinity,
> you, whom he in life doth hold,
> you, for whom himself was sold,
> you, on whom he still doth wait,
> whom he again would create;
> made by him, and purchased, why,
> why will you forever die?

Verse six addresses those nominal Christians of the English cities and countryside, who—having been exposed to the riches of the Christian tradition in Scripture and worship—have *not yet committed* themselves in covenant with the God who bids them to accept the inheritance that awaits them as sons and daughters of God.

> You, who own his record true,
> you, his chosen people, you,
> you, who call the Saviour Lord,
> you, who read his written Word,
> you, who see the gospel light,
> claim a crown in Jesus right;
> why will you, ye Christians, why
> will the house of Israel die?

This portrait of God as wooing English church folks ("house of Israel") to return to their *truest identity* as children of God serves as a good image for how the Wesleyan rule of life for spiritual formation imaged people turning from "the wrath to come" and learning to live according to the "gospel light" provided by the means of grace or ordinances.

WEEK ONE

A Prayer for the Church in Mission

Merciful God, may we love you with a whole heart;

May we always seek your face and find in you the joy of serving others.

May we discover the depths of your grace as we attend to that rule of life that draws us ever closer to you—
Hear our prayers, living God, for the life of your church and for your people everywhere.

Hear our prayers especially for the ministries of our conference and churches that they may communicate your compassionate presence to a world in need:
For ministries of mercy that express hope . . .
For ministries of piety that express faith . . .
For ministries of justice that demonstrate love-in-action . . .

Lord, hear our prayers and apply the benefits of your saving grace in Christ to our lives this day. Amen.

SUNDAY: DAY ONE

RE-ENGAGING THE GENERAL RULES

We embody the Wesleyan way of salvation as we commit ourselves to follow Christ (1) *by doing no harm . . . such as* **profaning the day of the Lord;** (2) *by doing good; of every possible sort . . .* **by clothing the naked;** *and* (3) by using the ordinary means of grace that God has given: **the public worship of God.**

Fifteen years ago, our friends Augie and Aimee Twigg, a United Methodist clergy couple in Western Pennsylvania, gave our family a small, handmade gift for Christmas. It is a framed copy of John Wesley's Rule: *"Do all the good you can, by all the means you can, in all the places you can, at all the times you can, to all the people you can, as long as ever you can."* This is one of those gifts that we treasure not only because our friends made it, but also because it reminds us of the covenant that we share with United Methodists around the world. We still keep it in a prominent place in our family room where it can be seen by all who enter.

Making gifts for friends was a tradition for the Twigg family. I imagine the pair of them making these gifts while relaxing on Sunday afternoons in Advent following a morning of preaching and leading public worship at the two sets of two-church "charges" that they served. Over the years, Aimee and Augie involved their children Andy and Addie in the creation of these gifts. Augie would do the calligraphy, Addie and Andy would press the flowers, and Aimee would assemble the calligraphy and flowers in a glass frame.

The Twiggs also tried to be disciplined about what kinds of activities they chose not to do on the Christian Sabbath day. Andy and Addie grew up knowing that Sundays were first and foremost for the purpose of gathering with other Christians for worship.

They learned that some activities were not appropriate to be done on Sundays; at the same time they grew up seeing how exceptions were made to deal with human needs. What the Twiggs stressed, in ordering daily life in their household, were the many positive ways in which keeping Sabbath offered their family opportunities for rest and recreation in the midst of their parents' active ministries.

This kind of positive focus *on what can be done* with our Sabbath time in contrast to those activities that do not honor the Lord's Day signals that Wesleyan Rule of Life is fundamentally about having our imaginations rightly ordered by the Gospel. "Clothing the naked" is one of the traditional "works of mercy" that Christians are called to do throughout their lives. Wesley emphatically stressed that if the works of mercy should conflict with the "works of piety," then one should let concern for one's neighbor take precedence. At the same time, Wesley admonished those who tried to evade Sabbath discipline out of a misplaced zeal for the gospel.

For many United Methodists, "John Wesley's Rule" serves as a memorable way to keep in mind the extensive nature of our calling as disciples of Jesus Christ. The gift that we received from our friends serves as a reminder for members of the Cartwright family that when we have imaginations shaped by keeping Sabbath, then we are more likely to display wisdom in knowing how to carry out the works of mercy.

DAILY WORD

Let love be genuine; hate what is evil; hold fast to what is good. . . . If your enemies are hungry, feed them; if they are thirsty give them something to drink. . . . Do not overcome evil with evil, but overcome evil with good. (Romans 12:9, 20-21)

PRAYER

O Lord, fill us with your love that we may share that love with others. Amen.

MONDAY: DAY TWO

RE-ENGAGING THE GENERAL RULES

We have covenanted with one another to follow Christ (1) **by doing no harm, such as taking of the name of God in vain**; (2) **by doing good**; by being in every kind merciful after their power; (3) by using the ordinary means of grace that God has given: [giving and receiving counsel or Christian Conference].

The practice of engaging in Christian conference—or "giving and receiving counsel" as it is sometimes called—is not as familiar in the 21st century as it was for the early Methodists. This may have something to do with the ways in which cynicism and sentimentality have captured our imaginations. According to Oscar Wilde, a *cynic* is someone "who knows the price of everything and the value of nothing." By contrast a *sentimental* person "values too many things but does not grasp the cost of anything." Wilde understood that ascribing value indiscriminately to persons or things makes us incapable of recognizing those things that are truly important.

Both cynicism and sentimentality can result in "taking the Lord's name in vain." Neither habit of mind displays careful speech. As a result, it is not only possible to "take the Lord's name in vain" by trivializing God; we also can act (like cynics) *as if it is not possible* to "do all the good we can," thereby denying our capacities to serve God in the world. Both patterns of behavior distract us from the gospel mandate to be merciful to others, *including our enemies* (Romans 12:19-21). However, in a world dominated by market-driven exchanges, those of us who seek to be merciful are apt to feel overwhelmed by the prospect that we are likely to be "taken advantage of" by our neighbors if we practice being merciful. This is one of the reasons it is helpful to talk about such quandaries with those who share our commitment to live our lives in the context of a covenant with God ordered by a rule of life for spiritual formation.

Valuing possessions and people *in the right ways at the right times for the right reasons* requires disciplined accountability to God. It also can help if we are willing to listen carefully to the counsel available from our brothers and sisters in Christ with whom we share the covenant. This is doubly important. As we make ourselves vulnerable to others by confessing our failings, we learn to be accountable to one another. At the same time, as we discover the forbearance that these brothers and sisters in Christ have shown us and realize how careful they have spoken to us, we can be encouraged to be more careful in the ways that we speak with others. When we give and receive counsel with brothers and sisters in Christ, we have the opportunity to encourage one another and we can be inspired to exercise imaginations that have been tutored by the good news of Jesus Christ. We also discover the humbling privilege of being able to "watch over one another in love" for the sake of the Gospel of Jesus Christ.

DAILY WORD

I therefore, the prisoner in the Lord, beg you to lead a life worthy of the calling to which you have been called, with all humility and gentleness, with patience, bearing with one another in love. (Ephesians 2:1-2)

PRAYER

O God, forgive us our cynicism and sentimentalism; help us to lead the life worthy of our calling in Christ. Amen.

TUESDAY: DAY THREE

RE-ENGAGING THE GENERAL RULES

It is expected of all who continue in these societies that they should continue to evidence their desire of salvation (1) **by doing no harm, by avoiding evil of every kind, such as drunkenness**; (2) **by doing good as they have opportunity**; (3) **by using the ordinary means of grace**: *the ministry of the Word, either read or expounded.*

John and Charles Wesley were Anglican priests whose minds were shaped by Scripture. Not surprisingly, the hymns that they wrote were filled with biblical allusions and images, and they both labored diligently in crafting sermons that applied the word of God to everyday life.

As Protestant Christians, they felt that it was the responsibility of every Christian to read and understand the Scriptures as well as to pay close attention to those clergy and laity who were gifted with the ability to explain the writings of Holy Scripture. At the same time, the brothers Wesley were well-educated "Oxford dons" who had the privilege of living at a time when the writings of the early church were being rediscovered.

For them, the ministry of the word included the commentaries associated with the "golden chain" of biblical interpretation. They encouraged their followers to take advantage of every opportunity to participate in the ministry of the word. Indeed it is not too much to say that John Wesley wanted Methodists to follow the apostolic mandate: "Let the word of Christ dwell in you richly" (Colossians 3:16).

According to John and Charles Wesley, to possess the kind of imagination that is alert to all possible opportunities for doing good that come our way is one of the marks of mature Christian living. Christian disciples must not find themselves numb or insensible to the word of God in their lives. Rather, they must exercise their responsibilities as "scribes of the kingdom" (Matt. 13:52) who have learned to exercise the kind of discerning judgment that would know when to bring forth treasures new and old from the storehouse for the purpose of bearing witness to the Gospel in the world. It follows, then, that early Methodists would not condone behaviors that would render them unable to respond to opportunities for doing good that God might place in their path.

This included the habit of drunkenness. Excessive consumption of alcohol takes place for various reasons, but it is avoidable. Wesley's concerns about the use of alcohol were not limited to drunkenness (see commentaries for days four and five), but he was clear that "getting drunk" was fundamentally incompatible with Christian discipleship in several ways.

First, someone who has indulged his or her appetite for alcohol to excess is not going to be alert to the possibilities of serving God in his or her daily life. More generally, drunkenness displays the kind of foolish behavior that in the parables of Jesus is associated with failing to be alert to the "in-breaking" of the Kingdom of God in our midst. When we take the time to watch over one another in love, we are not going to have time to get drunk, but we might discover that we have more opportunities for doing good than we might have thought we had.

DAILY WORD

Let the word of Christ dwell in you richly; teach and admonish one another in all wisdom; and with gratitude in your hearts sing psalms, hymns, and spiritual songs to God. (Colossians 3:16)

PRAYER

O Lord, may your Word take up residence in our hearts that we may worthily worship your holy name. Amen.

WEDNESDAY: DAY FOUR

RE-ENGAGING THE GENERAL RULES

It is expected of all who continue in these societies that they should continue to evidence their desire of salvation (1) *by doing no harm, by avoiding evil of every kind, such as* **buying or selling spirituous liquors;** (2) *by doing good; by* **doing good of every possible sort, and, as far as possible, to all men;** (3) *by attending upon all the ordinances of God:* **the Supper of the Lord.**

The great Reformer John Calvin regarded preaching as the "audible" form of the Word of God, and the Lord's Supper as the "visible" form of the Word of God. John Wesley would have phrased it differently, but there is good reason to believe that he thought along the same lines. Over the course of his lifetime, Wesley participated in the Eucharist an average of once every four days. Not surprisingly, Wesley urged members of the Methodist societies to participated in the Eucharist as often as they had opportunity to do so (see his sermon on "Constant Communion), and he believed that such participation would encourage faithful discipleship as ordinary men and women participated in the public liturgy of dying and being raised with Christ.

Wesley also advocated "doing good" in the most imaginative ways possible, including but not limited to economic sharing (see "Day Five" below) with others. Wesley's so-called "rule" on the use of money is an example: *"Earn all you can, save all you can, give all you can."* Later in his life, he would look on the growing wealth of Methodist people with strong disapproval, and regret that more had not followed this aspect of the Wesleyan rule of life.

The prohibition against buying and selling "spirituous liquors" was rooted in the early Methodist commitment to stand in solidarity with poor people. In the context of the Industrial Revolution and the growing urbanization of England, many people in the 18th century sought refuge from the abuses of the workplace in the new forms of distilled alcohol. While the analogy is somewhat imperfect, we might think of the ways in which poor people have sought refuge in cheap drugs like crack cocaine and "meth" (methamphetimines) in our own day. It is unthinkable that contemporary United Methodists would condone the use of crack cocaine when it is wreaking havoc in the lives of addicts.

While early Methodist societies were committed to standing in solidarity with those whose lives were being wrecked by spirituous liquors, they did not claim to be "teetotal" in their advocacy of temperance. In fact, it is a well-documented fact that early Methodists used wine in their celebrations of the Lord's Supper. Of greater concern to Wesley and participants in the Methodist societies and class meetings was how money was being used, and whether Methodists were sharing their financial resources with others. Later, Wesley would implement the use of "communion tickets" as a way of indicating those persons who were known to be living a life of holiness as described in the General Rules. It is why cultivating rich imaginations *about all the ways we can do* good remains an ongoing challenge for disciples in the 21st century. In that respect, we need the Eucharist *no less* than the first generation of Methodists.

DAILY WORD

For we are what he has made us, created in Christ Jesus for good works, which God prepared beforehand to be our way of life. (Ephesians 2:10)

PRAYER

O God, fill us with your goodness that we may visibly bring forth that goodness in the world. Amen.

THURSDAY: DAY FIVE

RE-ENGAGING THE GENERAL RULES

*It is expected of all who continue in these societies that they should continue to evidence their desire of salvation; (1) by doing no harm, by avoiding evil of every kind, such as **drinking** [spirituous liquors], **except in cases of extreme necessity;** (2) by doing good; **to all men, to their bodies**; (3) by attending upon all the ordinances of God: **family and private prayer**.*

Although the phrase "family and private prayer" may seem rather generic to 21st-century readers, the practice meant something rather precise for Wesley. As Ted Campbell has explained in his book *John Wesley and Christian Antiquity*, John Wesley associated the tradition of praying the daily office or "hours of prayer" with the practices of the early Church, particularly the gatherings in the Temple at the third, sixth, and ninth hours of each day—a practice that individual Christians continued through the third century. He also regarded this practice as one of the practices that linked early Methodism with "the whole Church in the purest ages." Although there is no evidence that Wesley ever read the *Rule of St. Benedict*, as an Anglican priest he was heir to the practice of morning and evening prayer as well as Compline or "night prayer," and his diaries display the ways that he maintained this practice throughout his lifetime.

Wesley also followed the ancient tradition of practicing the "corporal" (bodily) works of mercy: feeding the sick, visiting those in prison, feeding the hungry, etc. This explicit emphasis on practices that ministered to the bodies of those in need is an important feature of the communal character of early Methodist spirituality. It also meant that as Methodists consumed food and enjoyed good health and the freedoms of daily living, they did so in the awareness that other people were suffering and needed to be released from their captivity to various forms of evil "as most generally practiced."

In this way, the positive rules were reinforced by the specificity of those pursuits that Methodists renounced in the interest of bringing salvation to all.

Under the influence of the Temperance movement, many American Methodists came to read the General Rules as if drinking all forms of alcohol was strictly forbidden, but this was not the case (see "Day Four" above). Neither did John Wesley and the people called Methodists think that mere moderation was an adequate witness. Medical necessity was an acceptable reason for making an exception, but otherwise drinking whiskey, gin, vodka, and other forms of distilled alcohol was forbidden (even in the context of one's home and family) precisely because of the ways these forms of consumption distracted from keeping the needs of the poor in view. In these respects, early Methodism refused to permit abstractions to creep into their daily practice.

By showing restraint in one's personal consumption at the same time that one reaches out to minister to the "bodily needs" of others, John Wesley believed that "true Christian" men and women continually reminded themselves of the needs of others and God's work in the world. Prayer provided the necessary rhythm for lifting up these needs before God as well as reflecting on the ways God was calling for Christians to act upon the known needs of those around them.

DAILY WORD

When you are praying, do not heap up empty phrases as the Gentiles do; for they think that they will be heard because of their many words. Do not be like them, for your Father knows what you need before you ask him. (Matthew 6:7-8)

PRAYER

Counsel us by your grace, O Lord that we might offer ourselves in praise and thanksgiving to Jesus Christ our Savior. Amen.

FRIDAY: DAY SIX

RE-ENGAGING THE GENERAL RULES

United by God's grace, we commit ourselves to the way of discipleship (1) *by doing no harm, by avoiding evil of every kind, such as **fighting, quarreling, brawling, brother going to law with brother**;* (2) *by doing good, as far as possible, to all men: **to their bodies, of the ability which God giveth**;* (3) *by attending upon all the ordinances of God: **fasting or abstinence**.*

For several years, the two United Methodist clergy with whom I had formed a covenant group in the early 1990s kept a Friday fast at midday. Each of my colleagues lived forty miles from me (in different directions), so for practical reasons we found it difficult to gather on a weekly basis. Having resolved to meet twice a month, we agreed to hold one another in prayer during the intervening weeks and we committed ourselves to fasting for the same time period on Fridays. During that time we would reflect on portions of the Sermon on the Mount (Matt. 5-7). In addition to the fact that fasting provided an opportunity to break from our daily work responsibilities and refocus our attention on prayer, each of us took courage from knowing that the other two also were reflecting on the same passage of scripture while we abstained from lunch.

The means of grace known as fasting or abstinence is a practice often isolated from corporate practices, but however personal (and therefore "corporal") abstinence from eating and drinking may be, this particular gospel ordinance has a communal dimension. Traditionally, Christians have fasted on Fridays. John and Charles Wesley were shaped by the Anglican pattern of fasting from Thursday evening until Friday afternoon at 3 o'clock. Wesley's own practice was to fast from Thursday evening to Friday afternoon at 3 p.m. as well as for a portion of the day on Wednesday of each week.

With some notable exceptions, American Methodists have usually chosen not to fast on Wednesday and Friday like their Anglican forebears. Nineteenth-century American Methodists, influenced by the Temperance movement, also tended to emphasize abstinence from alcohol more than they urged fasting from food. But for John and Charles Wesley, this was a matter of both/and, not either/or. All of which means that early Methodists had to discuss these matters and consider their consumption of food and alcohol and the ways personal habits sustained or inhibited their abilities to serve God. Sometimes it can be remarkably convenient not to be aware of the abilities that God has given us to do good; Wesley advocated the practice of self-examination so that Methodists would not deceive themselves about such matters.

For too many people living in the first decade of the 21st century, the word "quarrelsome" is an adjective that seems to go with the word "Christian." Wesley was enough of a Pietist that he wanted to minimize conflicts over doctrine, where they did not pertain to essential doctrines. At the same time, he thought that it was important to stand up for "true Christianity" in the face of particular kinds of objections. More detrimental were the petty conflicts that Christians allow to become more important than their common loyalty to the Kingdom of God.

DAILY WORD

But when you fast, put oil on your head and wash your face, so that your fasting may be seen not by others but by your Father who is in secret; and your Father who sees in secret will reward you. (Matthew 6:17-18)

PRAYER

O Christ, may we seek first your Kingdom and righteousness in prayer and fasting. Amen.

SATURDAY: DAY SEVEN

RE-ENGAGING THE GENERAL RULES

We embody the Wesleyan rule of life for spiritual formation (1) *by doing no harm, by avoiding evil of every kind, especially that which is most generally practiced, such as **returning evil for evil, or railing for railing;*** (2) *by doing good, **by giving food to the hungry***; (3) ***by attending upon all the ordinances of God: searching the scriptures.***

For John Wesley and "the people called Methodists," to "search the scriptures" involved "trying every doctrine to see whether it be of God" according to the model of the Jewish community at Berea described in the Acts of the Apostles, which is said to have "examined the scriptures every day to see if these things [about the Christian gospel] were so" (Acts 17:11).

While not unique to Methodists or the theology of John Wesley, the practice of "searching the Scriptures" does display that kind of ongoing quest for wisdom that was a specific feature of early Methodism. Recalling two references in the New Testament (John 5:39, Acts 17:11), this practice was closely associated with the gatherings for Christian conference in which brothers and sisters in Christ gave and received counsel in addition to the ways individual disciples engaged in "faith seeking understanding." In important respects, the consensus that informed the General Rules was the product of the collective efforts of searching the scriptures. As Wesley explained to Methodism's opponents, *"We are always open to instruction, willing to be wiser every day than we were before, and to change whatever we can change for the better."*

Methodists did not need to search very far in the scriptures of the New Testament to find that they had a mandate to feed the hungry. The text of Matthew 25:31-46 provided the only warrant required for ministering "unto the least of these" (Matthew 25: 40b) and sharing food with the hungry was one of the most obvious ways to engage in "works of mercy." Even so, they sometimes struggled to know how best to go about carrying out this mandate, and disagreements did arise. In such circumstances, Wesley urged them to "bear with" one another for the sake of the gospel.

The quaint phrase "railing for railing" pertains to the kind of chronic conflict that tends to erupt from time to time in religious reform movements. It was also a reminder that on those occasions when the Christian quest to glean wisdom from scripture results in the kind of squabbling that causes dissension, then this means of grace very likely has been distorted into an end in itself. Wesley constantly reminded the people called Methodists that such practices were to produce the fruit of the Spirit (Galatians 5).

When Christians find ways to be in conflict over such things as whether to set up a food bank, they need to ask themselves what the source of the conflict is. In some cases, it may spring from a reluctance to engage in the nitty-gritty tasks associated with the works of mercy. In some cases it may arise out of ignorance; not everyone has read Matthew 25:31-46! And in some cases, people may actually enjoy being conflictual. In all cases, to indulge in chronic conflict is to permit ourselves to be distracted from our calling to be a holy people.

DAILY WORD

But you are a chosen race, a royal priesthood, a holy nation, God's own people, in order that you may proclaim the mighty acts of him who called you out of darkness into his marvelous light. (1 Peter 2:9)

PRAYER

O God, bring forth in our lives the fruit of your Holy Spirit that we may proclaim in word and deed Christ's love for all. Amen.

PRAISING GOD WITH JOHN & CHARLES WESLEY

"Come, O Thou Traveler Unknown" (Nos. 386-387 in *The United Methodist Hymnal*) is one of the hymns that early Methodists sang with conviction. The hymn was written by Charles; John cited it in the obituary that he prepared for his brother. Based on the story of Jacob wrestling with the angel at the Jabbok River (Genesis 32:23-32), this hymn testifies to the ways God saves us from ourselves and reorients us so that we can discover the wonders of friendship with God.

1 Come, O thou Traveler Unknown,
   Whom still I hold, but cannot see!
   My company before is gone,
   And I am left alone with thee;
   With thee all night I mean to stay,
   And wrestle till the break of day.
   With thee all night I mean to stay,
   And wrestle till the break of day.

2 I need not tell thee who I am,
   My misery or sin declare;
   Thyself hast called me by my name,
   Look on thy hands, and read it there.
   But who, I ask Thee, who are thou?
   Tell me thy name, and tell me now.
   But who, I ask Thee, who are thou?
   Tell me thy name, and tell me now.

3 Yield to me now, for I am weak,
   But confident in self-despair!
   Speak to my heart, in blessings speak,
   Be conquered by my instant prayer:
   Speak, or thou never hence shalt move,
   And tell me if thy name is Love.
   Speak, or thou never hence shalt move,
   And tell me if thy name is Love.

4 'Tis Love! 'Tis Love! Thou diedst for me;
   I hear thy whisper in my heart.
   The morning breaks, the shadows flee,
   Pure Universal Love thou art;
   To me, to all, thy mercies move—
   Thy nature, and thy name, is Love.
   To me, to all, thy mercies move—
   Thy nature, and thy name, is Love.

The original version of this hymn by Charles Wesley had fourteen stanzas. In this longer version, the later stanzas describe the reorientation of the person who has entered into a new relationship with the God that the voice of the hymn addresses as "pure Universal Love."

WEEK TWO

A Prayer for the Church in Mission

Living God, speak to us the blessings of your Son Jesus Christ. In the power of your Holy Spirit, communicate to us your Word of grace and truth that we may lead holy and righteous lives. Sanctify us, we pray.

O Lord, as we share in ministry together, may we remember the work of this annual conference.

We pray for our bishop and for all those who serve on our conference staff.

We pray for our superintendents as they watch over the ministry of those who lead the life of your church.

We pray for elders and deacons whose commission it is to order the mission of the church.

We pray for those whose ministry is beyond the local church and who demonstrate the love of Christ.

We pray for those who serve overseas and who represent Christ through the annual conference in ministries of evangelism and mission.

Lord, for these persons and more we lift up our hearts and ask for the wisdom, protection, and power of your Holy Spirit to guide and lead. In Christ's name, we pray. Amen.

SUNDAY: DAY EIGHT

RE-ENGAGING THE GENERAL RULES

It is expected of all who continue in these societies that they should continue to evidence their desire of salvation (1) *by doing no harm, by avoiding evil of every kind, such as the profaning the day of the Lord,* **by doing ordinary work therein;** (2) *by doing good, especially to them that are of the household of faith;* (3) *by attending upon all the ordinances of God:* **the public worship of God.**

Several years ago, a diverse group of theologians gathered as part of a working group on Christian practices. The topic of discussion for that particular session was "keeping Sabbath." All parties to this conversation were in agreement that Christian Sabbath should be a time in which Christians gather for public worship of God, but they also admitted that they struggled to mark the difference between Sunday as "the Lord's Day" and the other six days of the week.

The convener of the conversation asked these thoughtful people to talk about why that was the case. Most acknowledged that they did not so much "keep" the Sabbath as they worked through it in various ways. Some had pastoral responsibilities. Others worked on scholarly articles, etc. When asked where they would have to begin if they were going to be more disciplined in this Christian practice, one of the theologians chuckled ruefully and said, "I guess I would have to start by not doing e-mail on Sunday."

Once upon a time, e-mail might not have been thought of as an example of "ordinary work," but today many people carry Blackberry devices so that they can be available at all times to send and receive e-mail messages. It serves as a contemporary symbol of the ways that work dominates our lives in ways that leave us unbalanced. By contrast, the Wesleyan rule of life restores a sense of balance through the rhythm of Sabbath rest that makes it possible for us to give ourselves in public worship.

For John Wesley and "the people called Methodists," the call to refrain from doing "ordinary work" on Sunday might be said to be a first step in their individual and collective resolve to keep Sabbath. With our perspectives restored about what is truly most important in life, we are in a better position to discern what "good" might be done throughout the week in our daily lives. It is also the case that doing good to those who are members of the "household of faith" becomes more viable when we have gathered with them often enough to know what their needs are, and to inquire about "how it is with their souls."

This may be especially important now that many people in congregations live as "religious commuters," worshipping at a church that is located elsewhere from where they work and play, go to school, or shop. Gathering for public worship, then, might even be said to be more important for learning about the needs of others in our midst, particularly if we also are going to open our circles to "watch over them in love."

DAILY WORD

Remember the Sabbath day, and keep it holy. . . . the seventh day is a Sabbath to the Lord your God. (Exodus 20:8, 10)

PRAYER

O Lord, in our Sabbath time with you may we receive your Spirit of peace. Amen.

MONDAY: DAY NINE

RE-ENGAGING THE GENERAL RULES

We embody the Wesleyan rule of life for spiritual formation (1) *by doing no harm, by avoiding evil of every kind, such as* **the buying or selling goods that have not paid the duty**; (2) *by doing good, as far as possible, to all men* **by visiting or helping them that are sick**; (3) *by attending upon all the ordinances of God:* [**Christian Conference or giving and receiving counsel**].

Giving and receiving counsel with one another includes questions about "the works of mercy" as well as "the works of piety." As I have noted in my comments on earlier sequences of the General Rules, early Methodists thought that conversations about money must include being candid when we are tempted to skirt the law of the land by either buying or selling products outside the framework of legal taxation.

At the personal level, some of us are often tempted to think that is justifiable to declare a (unilateral) "personal exemption" from the public "common good" that is being secured through whatever tariffs or taxes on purchases may exist. Those who own or manage businesses may seek "competitive advantage" by arranging transactions "under the table," thereby hiding the income gained from the Internal Revenue Service.

Those of us who have had the privilege of traveling to other nations have had the experience of "declaring" those items that we are bringing back into our native country. Not everything that we might like to designate "duty-free" is given that status by the nation-state in which we live or the countries that we may visit in our international travels for business or leisure purposes. In mandating that Methodists would not engage in this practice, John Wesley made it clear that "true Christians" should not attempt to disengage from the "common good," including those special taxes in which the economic needs of the commonwealth require forms of sacrifice from those individuals who have sufficient wealth to purchase items that are subject to "luxury taxes."

Visiting the sick is one of the traditional "works of mercy" that in many congregations is done only by the pastor or professionalized caregivers such as "parish nurses." Today, the practice of medicine is more and more geared toward "cure," and, increasingly, "care" is something that has to be purchased from various health care providers. Professions like home health care nursing and adult care as well as hospice or care at the end of life offer such care for a fee to those who have the means to pay.

United Methodists need to recover the practice of visiting or helping those who are sick or dying as a means of combating the social stratification by wealth. To care for the sick is to engage in a form of solidarity that should not be defined by wealth and privilege. To do so is also likely to produce questions and quandaries about the difference between "want" and "need," for which we will need the counsel of brothers and sisters in Christ who are committed to watching over one another in love.

DAILY WORD

Therefore confess your sins to one another, and pray for one another, so that you may be healed. The prayer of the righteous is powerful and effective. (James 5:16)

PRAYER

O God, Giver of life, heal us with the ointment of your grace that we might experience your wholeness and love. Amen.

TUESDAY: DAY TEN

RE-ENGAGING THE GENERAL RULES

As disciples of Jesus Christ, we watch over one another in love (1) *by doing no harm, by avoiding evil of every kind, such as **giving or taking things on usury—i.e., unlawful interest**;* (2) *by doing good, as far as possible, to all men **by visiting or helping them that are in prison**;* (3) *by attending upon all the ordinances of God:* **the ministry of the Word, either read or expounded.**

For the brothers Wesley and other "Methodists," the ministry of the Word was a practice that was intended to suffuse ordinary life. Like St. Paul, they wanted "the word of Christ to dwell in you richly" (Col. 3:16). As John Wesley's *Journal* shows, their experience was that over and over again reading Scripture on a daily basis and hearing others preach the word strengthened their resolve to do good and convinced them that their passivity about injustice could not be indulged.

The brothers Wesley visited those who were in prison, then, not because they pitied them but because they wanted to bear witness to the good news of the Gospel of Jesus Christ. "Extol the Lamb of God/the all-atoning lamb, redemption in his blood, throughout the world proclaim." Charles's hymn "Blow Ye, the Trumpet Blow" draws upon the jubilee tradition of Leviticus 25, Isaiah 60, and Luke 4:14-21 to render in poetry the liberating power of salvation in Christ. "Ye slaves of sin and hell/your liberty receive/and safe in Jesus dwell/and blest in Jesus live."

Imagine early Methodists singing with gusto in gatherings with prisoners who had experienced just what they were singing. At least some of the persons who would be imprisoned in eighteenth-century England would have received their sentence to a penitentiary not because they had committed a particular crime but simply because they had suffered great misfortune and were unable to pay their debts. English common law included provisions against "usury," thereby limiting some forms of injustice, but there were ways that persons could get around such laws through forms of informal exchange.

Contemporary United Methodists face a more complex scenario in the context of what some have called "late modern capitalism," an environment of banking commerce and personal finance in which some businesses make money by encouraging persons to go into debt through the use of credit cards.

It is not uncommon for some people to spend their entire lives in debt. Only vestiges of the old "usury laws" remain in place. While it is not as common for persons to be imprisoned for their debts as it was in Wesley's day, poverty and indebtedness remain. A contemporary restatement of the General Rules would probably have to include a longer list of injustices that perpetuate poverty through legalized gambling (euphemistically referred to as "gaming") and forms of "investment" that more and more resemble imprudent risk-taking for the thrill.

DAILY WORD

The Spirit of the word is upon me, because he has anointed me to bring good news to the poor. He has sent me to proclaim release to the captives and recovery of sight to the blind, to let the oppressed go free, to proclaim the year of the Lord's favor. (Luke 4:18-19)

PRAYER

O Lamb of God, who takes away the sins of the world redeem us by the power of your blood
that we may live at one with you and our neighbors. Amen.

WEDNESDAY: DAY ELEVEN

RE-ENGAGING THE GENERAL RULES

We have covenanted with one another to follow Christ (1) *by doing no harm, by avoiding evil of every kind, such as **uncharitable or unprofitable conversation; particularly speaking evil of magistrates or of ministers**;* (2) *by doing good, as far as possible, to all men **to their souls, by instructing** . . . ;* (3) *by attending upon all the ordinances of God: **the Supper of the Lord.***

Participation in the Lord's Supper calls on Christians to be reconciled with one another even when we find it difficult to bear with one another. Part of what is involved when clergy and laity gather to offer the "Great Thanksgiving" is to acknowledge all that God has provided—including one another. In times of conflict, pastors may not be so sure that we want to give God thanks and praise for "Mrs. McGillicuddy"—an inveterate gossip who seems to have perfected the art of making the most mischief with the least trustworthy bits of gossip—or "Old Joe Motes"—that well-intended but undiscerning soul whose ideological commitment to some cause perpetually seems to threaten the health of congregational life with a narrow agenda that conveniently ignores his own personal practices.

Similarly, as the laity gather around the table for the Eucharist with their pastor, they may be on edge about the pastor's latest "proposal" for how to transform the congregation and bring the Kingdom of God (before he or she moves on to a bigger appointment)—a pattern that they had seen too often over the years.

During the two years that I served as a rural pastor, I quickly discovered that if I did not take proactive action at the beginning of each week, a sharp-tongued woman in the congregation would unintentionally start several "brush fires" that would take time to put out. I decided that rather than have the grapevine operate to a deadly effect, I would try to get a "good humor wagon" going by calling "Alberta" and spending a few minutes talking with her on Monday morning of each week. We would discuss the previous day's events and I would listen to her complaints and remind her of the good things that were happening that we should celebrate. Usually, three or four days later, word got back to me about what Alberta was saying about all the good things that were happening, a judgment that, amazingly, others seemed to share.

While I was aware of the dangers (condescension, etc.) involved with my pastoral intervention, I genuinely enjoyed my weekly conversations with Alberta, and I also thought that I had a responsibility as her pastor to teach her more edifying forms of Christian conversation. Over time, I discovered that this elderly woman became a very effective ambassador of "good news" for the congregation, and contributed to our ability to celebrate what God was doing in our life together as a church.

At the same time, she learned to assert her concerns to me, knowing that I would listen to her admonitions as well as instruct her when she started going overboard. While clergy and laity certainly need to exercise prudence in how we choose to instruct one another, we cannot let the social pressure to be nice derail us from the common endeavor that we share as disciples of Jesus Christ. Most of all, we need to give thanks for one another as we gather at the table that the Lord has prepared for all of us.

DAILY WORD

So, whether you eat or drink, or whatever you do, do everything for the glory of God. Give no offense to Jews or to Greeks or to the church of God, just as I try to please everyone in everything I do, not seeking my own advantage, but of many, so that they may be saved. (1 Cor. 10:32-33)

PRAYER

O God, give us this day our daily bread, and forgive us our trespasses as we forgive those who trespass against us. Amen.

THURSDAY: DAY TWELVE

RE-ENGAGING THE GENERAL RULES

We embody the Wesleyan rule of life for spiritual formation (1) *by doing no harm, by avoiding evil of every kind, such as **doing to others as we would not they should do unto us**;* (2) *by doing good, as far as possible, to all men **to their souls**, by reproving all we have any intercourse with*; (3) *by attending upon all the ordinances of God: **family and private prayer**.*

The practice of daily prayer, personally and with members of our family, provides us with an opportunity to "sit with" our inclinations to engage others about issues that have arisen between us. At Night Prayer, this may mean that as I reflect on the day's events, I realize that I spoke too sharply to one of my children, or my spouse, or a colleague at work, and in the context of self-examination, I resolve to go to that person and work through the conflict by taking responsibility for not responding in the best way. It may also mean that I begin to recognize a need to speak with someone about a matter that I have noticed but have been tempted to ignore because I did not want to have to deal with the conflict that might erupt if I serve as an advocate for the custodian who was berated and embarrassed in front of co-workers by a manager in a circumstance in which a simple reminder would have been sufficient.

I would hope that Christians would exercise great caution before we attempt to "reprove" strangers or persons we encounter in the midst of daily living at work or during our travels. While there are plenty of injustices and inappropriate behaviors that we are likely to encounter, it is all too easy to go off half-cocked in the midst of misperceiving a given situation. At the same time, we are called to serve as ambassadors of a ministry of reconciliation (2 Cor. 5:18-20), and that will certainly require offering reproof to those who are bent on fostering dissension and ill will in spheres great or small. Part of discerning how to speak in disciplined ways involves sorting out the source of the authority of the word that we might bear to others we encounter, and therefore speaking in a manner in accord with the word that is authorized by the gospel. *"Stand therefore, and fasten the belt of truth around your waist. . . . As shoes for your feet put on whatever will make you ready to proclaim the gospel of peace"* (Ephesians 6:15-16).

Here it seems to me that practicing the "golden rule" can serve as well in many instances as we attempt to sort out whether to call attention to someone else's errors. By logical extension, if we stop to think about whether we would want someone else to do to us what we are about to do to them, then, we might also recall Jesus' parable about the need to remove the "mote" from our own eye before we try to remove the log from our brother or sister's eye.

The Wesleyan Rule of Life calls on us to seek the balance of speaking the truth in love to all we encounter, even as we attempt to hear the word of truth in the rhythm of daily prayer that convicts us of our own sins.

DAILY WORD

All this is from God, who reconciled himself to us through Christ, and has given us the ministry of reconciliation. (2 Cor. 5:18)

PRAYER

O God, may we serve as ambassadors of your reconciliation, giving you thanks for the forgiveness of sins and offering praise for the Light of salvation. Amen.

FRIDAY: DAY THIRTEEN

RE-ENGAGING THE GENERAL RULES

United by God's grace, we commit ourselves to the way of discipleship (1) *by doing no harm, by avoiding evil of every kind, such as **doing what we know is not for the glory of God**;* (2) *by doing good, as far as possible, to all men, **to their souls, by exhorting all we have any intercourse with**;* (3) by practicing the ordinary means of grace as God has given: ***fasting or abstinence.***

Abstinence is a discipline that refocuses our attention. Doing without food helps reorient us to the needs of our body as well as the needs of those around us. When we abstain from food on Friday, it helps to focus our attention on the paschal mystery; i.e. what it means for each of us to die and be raised with Christ.

To fast and/or abstain from certain forms of food and drink once a week, then, helps us to mark time by engaging in acts of repentance (as we may do also on special days like Ash Wednesday and Good Friday). It also may serve as a way of focusing on the mission of the Church. For example, members of *The Ekklesia Project*, an ecumenical network of pastors, theologians, and other advocates of radical discipleship, have covenanted to pray for renewal of the church every Friday at midday.

The phrase "doing what we know is not for the glory of God" seems to have served as an appeal to personal conscience for John Wesley and the people called Methodists. As Chapter 14 of Paul's letter to the Romans reminds us, attempting to apply a standard of incongruity with gospel practices can result in disagreements between persons of weaker or more robust conscience. But as we lift up this higher standard of behavioral expectations for one another (beyond the expectations of conventional behavior or common decency), we help to cultivate an ethos in United Methodist covenant groups and even congregations in which we seek to glorify God in all things. This is also why we would dare to exhort one another, because we understand ourselves as sharing a covenant (see pp. 55-56 for covenant prayer).

Exhortation was one of the forms that lay leadership took in early Methodism. An exhorter might add his or her word of encouragement or admonition after the circuit-riding preacher had offered a sermon, or, in the absence of an appointed preacher, a gathering of a Methodist "society" or "class meeting" might read one of John Wesley's published sermons and then add thoughts about how to apply what had been expounded to the daily lives of those gathered.

Exhortation sometimes takes the form of admonishing fellow Christians for being over-scrupulous or for misguided forms of Christian spiritual disciplines. Someone who fails to keep in mind that fasting and abstinence are located within a rhythm of life in which it is also appropriate to have "soul feasts" might need to receive exhortation for excessive emphasis on such disciplines.

DAILY WORD

Welcome one another, therefore, just as Christ has welcomed you, for the glory of God. (Romans 14:7)

PRAYER

Glory to you, O Lord, for the love you have poured into our hearts by the power of your Holy Spirit! We praise your name! Amen.

SATURDAY: DAY FOURTEEN

RE-ENGAGING THE GENERAL RULES

We have covenanted with one another to follow Christ (1) *by doing no harm, by avoiding evil of every kind, such as* **the using [of] many words in buying or selling**; (2) *by doing good, as far as possible, to all men* **by trampling under foot that enthusiastic doctrine that "we are not to do good unless <u>our hearts be free to it</u>"**; (3) *by attending upon all the ordinances of God:* **searching the Scriptures.**

Searching the Scriptures was a corporate discipline, a feature of early Methodism that is reflected in the very fact that the "General Rules of the United Societies" came to exist in documentary form in the first place. As Methodist societies in Bristol and London and elsewhere came to consensus about how to live their lives by doing no harm and by doing good as much as possible to all people, they began to put their collective wisdom together in *Books of Doctrine and Discipline*, which in the earliest editions were closer to being manuals for spiritual formation than they were for organizational structure. These little volumes also contained what amounts to extended commentaries on significant portions of Scripture. For example, on various occasions Wesley argued that the "general rules of the united societies" were little more than a contemporary restatement of the substance of Jesus' Sermon on the Mount.

By contrast, one of the earliest forms of opposition that Wesley and company faced in the context of the English Evangelical Revival was a form of "quietism" associated with the Moravians and related Pietist groups that taught that in the absence of any particular personal promptings of the Holy Spirit, "true Christians" should do nothing. John Wesley sternly opposed this "enthusiastic doctrine" that was particularly dangerous precisely because of the ways it ignored traditions of Christian spirituality such as the "works of mercy" and the "works of piety." Wesley believed that the "ordinary means of grace" were part of God's providence to be followed in the absence of any extraordinary directives that Methodists might discover.

"Searching the Scriptures" also led the people called Methodists to be careful about their speech by "taming the tongue" (James 3:1-12). John Wesley and early Methodists would not have been quite as rigorous about the use of words in commercial transactions as the English Quakers were known to be at that time, but even so, they would have urged one another to exercise caution in the ways in which they used language in buying and selling material goods. Then as now, it is possible for a "slick-talking" salesperson to deceive someone about a product. Also, in the eighteenth century, literacy was still a form of privilege; those who could read, therefore, were in a position to use words as tools to take advantage of those who were illiterate.

DAILY WORD

You are the light of the world. A city built on a hill cannot be hid. No one after lighting a lamp puts it under the bushel basket, but on the lampstand, and it gives light to all in the house. In the same way, let your light shine before others, so that they may see your good works and give glory to your Father in heaven. (Matthew 5:14-16)

PRAYER

O God, may your renewing Spirit open our hearts and minds to your Word that we may proclaim your truth in love. Amen.

PRAISING GOD WITH JOHN & CHARLES WESLEY

"Blow Ye, The Trumpet Blow" (#379 *The United Methodist Hymnal*) is a hymn that proclaims the victory of God over sin and death and invites "ransomed sinners" to return home to the God who saves.

Blow ye the trumpet, blow!
The gladly solemn sound
Let all the nations know,
To earth's remotest bound;

Refrain:
The year of jubilee is come!
The year of jubilee is come!
Return, ye ransomed sinners, home.

Jesus, our great high priest,
Hath full atonement made;
Ye weary spirits rest;
Ye mournful souls, be glad.
Refrain

Extol the Lamb of God,
The all-atoning Lamb;
Redemption in his blood
Throughout the world proclaim:
Refrain

Ye slaves of sin and hell,
Your liberty receive,
And safe in Jesus dwell,
And blest in Jesus live:
Refrain

Ye who have sold for nought
Your heritage above
Shall have it back unbought,
The gift of Jesus' love:
Refrain

The gospel trumpet hear,
The news of heavenly grace;
And saved from earth appear
Before your Savior's face:
Refrain

As this hymn once sung by our Methodist mothers and fathers reminds us, we enjoy freedom from sin and so we join them in giving thanks by offering hymns of praise to the God who saves.

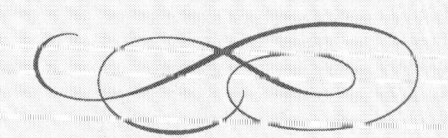

BELIEVE · LOVE · OBEY

WEEK THREE

A Prayer for the Church in Mission

Almighty God, revive us again through the power of your Holy Spirit! Renew us by the grace of Jesus Christ and create in us a new heart that we perfectly magnify your holy name.

O God, form in us the life-giving love of Jesus Christ and help us to see the moving of your Spirit in the church and world.

Shape in us the mercy revealed on the cross and reveal to us the mission of your kingdom among those who are left out and forgotten.

Lord, as we pray for the renewal of your church may we remember the faithful ministries that call people into a relationship with Jesus Christ. Help us to realize that renewal is taking place and that we have been called to share in that work:

For ministries of renewal: The Walk to Emmaus, Academy for Spiritual Formation, Covenant Discipleship, the Upper Room, the Disciple Bible Study, Volunteers in Mission, Operation Classroom, Work Teams, and more.

Lord, remind us that you don't leave us without the treasures of hope and renewal. Amen.

SUNDAY: DAY FIFTEEN

RE-ENGAGING THE GENERAL RULES

We embody the Wesleyan rule of life for spiritual formation (1) by doing no harm, by avoiding evil of every kind, such as **profaning the day of the Lord or by buying or selling**; *(2) by doing good, as far as possible, to all men especially to them that are of the household of faith . . .* **by all possible frugality, that the gospel be not blamed**; *(3) by attending upon all the ordinances of God:* **the public worship of God.**

When I was in graduate school, my upstairs neighbor once told me that in his experience most Protestant Christians seemed to worship money more than God. While I did not share his assessment of what was really going on when Christian congregations "take an offering" and then sing a "doxology," I had to wince at the ways he could make it sound as if we are doing the very opposite of what we claim that we are doing when we gather for the public worship of God. My neighbor was a graduate student in English literature, and in retrospect, I think he probably had a habit of "deconstructing" everything his eyes set upon regardless of what kind of text he encountered. Unfortunately, my neighbor is not the only "cultivated cynic" that I have encountered who is eager to call attention to the ways Christians can be seen to "profane the day of the Lord" in various kinds of "public" activities, including buying and selling things.

As John Howard Yoder taught us in many of his essays and books, Christians need to remember that we live our lives "before the eyes of the watching world," and therefore virtually all that we say and do can be thought of as *some form of Christian witness* (however deficient or excellent our actions may be) whether we intend it as such or not. In other words, those of us who claim to be Christians cannot afford the self-deception of thinking that our mundane actions on Sunday (or any other day of the week) can be dismissed because we are content to have satisfied our obligation to worship God. Such "privatization" of our loyalty to God is self-deceived at best. In our time, "not being conformed to this world" includes the time and date of our consumption patterns, and "presenting our bodies as living sacrifices, wholly and acceptable to God" entails more than placing a check in the offering plate. It involves "discerning what is the will of God, what is good, acceptable and perfect." (Romans 12:1-2)

Wesley was famously frugal with his money, and many early Methodists did follow the rule of "earn all you can, give all you can, save all you can." The addition of the words "that the gospel be not blamed" is a telling reminder that one of the ways that Christian witness can be damaged is by undisciplined uses of money. Frugality, then, was understood in relation to the objective of doing everything in ways that glorified God on Sunday as well as throughout the rest of the week.

DAILY WORD

I appeal to you therefore, brothers and sisters, by the mercies of God, to present your bodies as a living sacrifice, holy and acceptable to God, which is your spiritual worship. Do you not be conformed to this world, but be transformed by the renewing of your minds, so that you may discern what is the will of God—what is good and acceptable and perfect. (Romans 12:1-2)

PRAYER

O Lord, transform the thoughts of our minds by the inspiration of your Holy Spirit that we may love you and worthily magnify your holy name. Amen.

MONDAY: DAY SIXTEEN

RE-ENGAGING THE GENERAL RULES

As disciples of Jesus Christ, we watch over one another in love (1) *by doing no harm, by avoiding evil of every kind, such as doing what we know is not for the glory of God,* as **putting on of gold and costly apparel**; (2) *by doing good as far as possible, to all men **especially to them that are of the household of faith***; (3) by practicing the means of grace that God has already given to us: **[Christian Conference or giving and receiving counsel]**.

When done well, the practice of giving and receiving counsel probes into our daily lives in ways that—however uncomfortable it may be at a given moment—convey the loving concern of those who dare to care for us. In this respect, "watching over one another in love" has a stereoscopic dimension. On the one hand, we are aware of the fact that others are bound by the covenant commitment that we share in ways that require that they take seriously concerns and counsel that we may have to offer to them.

At the same time, we are aware of our responsibility to them (as defined in the context of the covenant we share) to offer counsel where we are in a position to do so. This does not mean that Christians in covenant groups always have counsel to offer. There will be times when the only "wise counsel" we can bring may take the form of loving silence in which all parties refrain from speaking, in the awareness that they all need to discern how the Holy Spirit is moving in their midst.

Another reason why Christian counsel is important is that we cannot act as if our behaviors (personal or collective) are *irrelevant* to those who are enduring spiritual struggles or who have recently become members of the body of Christ and who may be vulnerable in ways that others may not be. The way we live our lives is a witness of one kind or another, and we should care enough for the "household of faith" in which we have the privilege of being members to live our lives in ways that "do good" to and for our brothers and sisters in Christ.

To locate "the putting on of gold and costly apparel" as an example of the kind of activity or behavior that "we know is not for the glory of God" is not so much to act like a Puritan or to give way to Victorian mores as it is to put our needs and wants into context with respect to the fact that "whether we live or whether we die, we live or we die unto the Lord." Early Methodists tended to dress in a plain and unadorned manner. It was a matter of great controversy in the 1870s when Bishop Matthew Simpson's wife began wearing jewelry.

During the first three decades of the twentieth century, many American Methodists became middle class. Today, Wesleyans associated with the Holiness movement probably pay more attention to this concern than do United Methodists. Although we can always identify examples of "narrow-minded thinking" about clothing and jewelry, it is also true that what we wear does display our care in the use of our money, as well as in our concern for the needs of others in the "household of faith" and beyond.

DAILY WORD

As God's chosen ones, holy and beloved, clothe yourselves with compassion, kindness, humility, meekness, and patience . . . above all, clothe yourselves with love, which binds everything together in perfect harmony. (Colossians 3:12, 14)

PRAYER

O God, may we put on the garments of love and compassion that the peace of Christ may rule in our hearts. Amen.

TUESDAY: DAY SEVENTEEN

RE-ENGAGING THE GENERAL RULES

It is expected of all who continue in these societies that they should continue to evidence their desire of salvation; (1) *by doing no harm, by avoiding evil of every kind, such as doing what we know is not for the glory of God, such as* **taking such diversions as cannot be used in the name of the Lord Jesus**; (2) *by doing good, as far as possible, to all men especially to them that are of the household of faith* **or groaning so to be; employing them preferably to others**; (3) *by using the ordinary means of grace:* **the ministry of the Word, either read or expounded.**

When I was in high school, I took a job in a shoe warehouse owned by Bill Hutcheson, a United Methodist layperson. At the time, it was not at all clear to Bill—or to me—that I would go on to become a United Methodist minister. Nor was it clear that I was stable in my Christian faith. In fact, it was a time of extraordinary change in my life, during which I struggled for stability as I tried to come to grips with my calling and my relationship with God. Over the next five years, Mr. Hutcheson made it possible for me to complete high school and college by providing opportunity for employment *any time* I happened to be in town. I do not know the basis of his judgment about this matter, but I do know that he was proud of his Methodist heritage and emphatic about the importance of seeking guidance from scripture both in the context of daily prayer and in thoughtfully engaging his pastor's sermons.

I don't know if Bill Hutcheson ever thought about employing me in relation to the statements in the General Rules, but I know he was aware that I needed encouragement. I was going to move from destructive behaviors toward a way of life patterned after the life, ministry, death, and resurrection of Jesus Christ. Later I did join the congregation where Bill and his family were members. To say United Methodists should employ those who either are part of the household of faith or who are "serious seekers" should not be interpreted as a justification for discriminatory prejudice. On the contrary, it should be taken as a mandate for the kind of reaching out to those on the margins that would require our congregations to be more hospitable to persons in need.

At different times, Christians have drawn the line between those diversions subject to Christian uses and those that were not "useful" in different ways, and God knows we have generated plenty of unimaginative and even utilitarian thinking. Here, we probably also need to learn to use a "logic of addition" in the way we think about how to help those who are coming into our "open circle" as opposed to a "logic of subtraction."

Had Bill Hutcheson chosen to do so, he could have imagined circumstances in which I would abuse the opportunities that he gave me and conceivably ruled me out as unlikely to be worth the effort. But Bill Hutcheson had enough experience helping wayward souls to have some sense of what might work with folks like me, and he chose to take the risk in the hope that his efforts might work with the Holy Spirit's activity in my life. It probably never occurred to him to think that I would become a United Methodist, but that was the risk that he took when he and others invited me to join the fellowship of "serious seekers" known as United Methodists.

DAILY WORD

Let mutual love continue. Do not neglect to show hospitality to strangers, for by doing that some have entertained angels without knowing it. (Hebrews 13:1-2)

PRAYER

O God, help us as servants of the living Christ to open our hands to welcome those who are seeking you, thereby extending your kingdom to all. Amen.

WEDNESDAY: DAY EIGHTEEN

RE-ENGAGING THE GENERAL RULES

*We follow the Wesleyan rule of life (1) by doing no harm, by avoiding evil of every kind, such as **taking of such diversions as cannot be used in the name of the Lord Jesus**; (2) by doing good, as far as possible, to all men, especially to them that are of the household of faith, **buying one of another**; (3) by attending upon all the ordinances of God: **the Supper of the Lord**.*

Membership in a Christian community can be as ordinary as sharing money and as profound as partaking in the Body and Blood of Christ in the Eucharist. Too often, the bonds of "community" are primarily sentimental and therefore weak and ineffectual. As a result, our economic exchanges tend to become dominated by self-interest, not by thanksgiving. But that need not be the case.

A Baptist congregation that I know holds its celebration of the Lord's Supper once a month on Sunday evening. During the service, the congregation passes the plate to collect an offering for the needs of the poor. The intent of the offering is that—one way or another—*all* of the funds from the offering that evening would be given to those in need. Persons at the gathering who had needs were encouraged to take money from the plate as it was passed around, and all those gathered were urged to give thanks to God for *the abundance of wealth that makes it possible for some members to give and some members to receive*. This monthly gathering also reminds the congregation to engage in the works of mercy within and beyond the congregation at other times as well.

When we practice the "works of mercy," Christians seek other means than the faceless forms of charity that shield us from the specter of poverty. In the "parish system" of the Church of England it was common for people to look to the British "commonwealth" for funding. John Wesley called upon Methodists to *go beyond* government aid to perform "works of mercy" associated with the "commonwealth of heaven" (Hebrews). In the process, the Methodist societies became centers of economic exchange in ways that actually redistributed funds within the fellowship. As Wendell Berry reminds us, part of what it means to be part of a "membership" is to participate in a "local economy." This is the scale John Wesley had in mind. Where Christians who "trade" with one another are committed to "give all they can," then the primary purpose of our economic exchanges does not have to be to maximize the profit.

All of this helps explain why John Wesley and the people called Methodists made "use in the name of Jesus Christ" as the principal criterion for judging which "diversions" were to be avoided and which could be enjoyed. Spending significant sums of money without respect for the well-being of others was frowned upon. What initially may seem to be a rather puritanical prohibition was actually a reminder to use their imaginations in ways that enable *all members of the Body* to reaffirm the Lordship of Jesus Christ over all of life, thereby refocusing our perceptions of how we are to enjoy ourselves with one another. Hosting a fellowship dinner to celebrate the graduation of the child of another member of the congregation can be an occasion to experience great joy even as one chooses to refrain from other forms of privatized entertainment that cannot be experienced with brothers and sisters in Christ.

DAILY WORD

For just as the body is one and has many members, and all the members of the body, though many, are many, so it is with Christ. For in the one Spirit we were all baptized into one body—Jews or Greeks, slaves or free—and we were all made to drink of one Spirit. (1 Cor. 12:12-13)

PRAYER

Lord of heaven and earth, increase our love of you that we show mercy in our work and charity in our witness to offer to others the joy of Christ. Amen.

THURSDAY: DAY NINETEEN

RE-ENGAGING THE GENERAL RULES

We live out the meaning of the Wesleyan Rule of life (1) *by doing no harm, by avoiding evil of every kind, especially that which is most generally practiced, such as doing what we know is not for the glory of God, as:* ***softness and needless self-indulgence***; (2) *by doing good, as far as possible, to all men, especially to them that are of the household of faith . . .* ***helping each other in business***; (3) *by attending upon all the ordinances of God:* ***family and private prayer.***

The four Cartwright teenagers stood in the cold with their parents awaiting the beginning of the "Drumstick Dash," a 2.5-kilometer walk. Parents and children alike would probably have preferred being at home watching the Macy's Thanksgiving Parade in anticipation of a huge meal later that afternoon. Having discerned that we needed to become more involved in ministries to homeless persons, however, on this holiday we managed to drag ourselves to the starting line. We still had the meal later in the day, but at least we had exercised vigorously earlier in the day—and in the process contributed over $100 to feed hungry homeless men and women in our city.

In a world marked by such divisions between private privilege and the needs of public realms, there is a real danger that the robust practice of family and private prayer John Wesley advocated might be misunderstood. By no means does Wesley think that the prayers of persons living in households should be disengaged from issues of public concern. To borrow Rodney Clapp's phrase, John Wesley would more nearly think of the family as a "mission base" from which to move out to engage a host of worldly concerns. To do, that of course will mean that families need to become more like an "open circle" and less like self-contented suburban cocoons.

Today, Wendell Berry is regarded as a counterculturural critic because he advocates "seceding" from the global economy at the same time that he encourages citizens to focus greater attention on creating and sustaining "local economies." Berry believes that part of the problem is that many people no longer grasp what it means to have "membership" in a community, nor do they see the manifold ways individual households help sustain one another through economic exchange that makes it viable for small farms to thrive.

In a culture in which therapeutic idioms are so common as to be clichés, it may be difficult for contemporary United Methodists to hear they should not do things out of dispositions of "softness and needless self-indulgence." Indeed, we dare not ignore the very real concerns about "self-care" that have emerged as we have started paying more attention to social patterns of "workaholism" and other addictive patterns of activity. At the same time, it is possible to make stable distinctions between acting like "couch potatoes" and getting the kind of exercise that makes us physically fit. In a world of self-preoccupation and isolating personal forms of entertainment (iPods are simply the latest form of a now well-established preference), Christian families not only need to pray together but also need to learn to work and play together, especially if parents and children alike are going to develop the capacity to practice "radical hospitality," much less learn to "watch over one another in love" in ways that will sustain the practice of speaking the truth to one another in love.

DAILY WORD

For you were called to freedom, brothers and sisters, only do not use your freedom as an opportunity for self-indulgence, but through love become servants to one another. For the whole law is summed up in a single commandment, "You shall love your neighbor as yourself." If, however, you bite and devour one another, take care that you are not consumed by one another. (Gal. 5:13-15)

PRAYER

Triune God, may our families only serve you to honor you in how we reach out to the least of these, our brothers and sisters. Amen.

FRIDAY: DAY TWENTY

RE-ENGAGING THE GENERAL RULES

United by God's grace, we commit ourselves to the way of discipleship (1) *by doing no harm, such as **laying up treasure upon earth***; (2) *by doing good, as far as possible, to all men, especially to them that are of the household of faith **and so much the more because the world will love its own and them only***; (3) *by practicing the means of grace that God has given: **fasting or abstinence**.*

For most Americans, the day following Thanksgiving brings with it the recognition that not only did we eat too much for dinner the previous day, but we are tempted to consume too much in other ways as well. Of course, not everyone enjoys shopping, but even those of us who do not engage in binge shopping probably have too much "stuff." At the same time, we are more and more preoccupied with various forms of "social security" and many around us are being downsized or losing pensions for retirement in the midst of marketplace changes. Meanwhile, virtually no one feels satisfied in the midst of insatiable patterns of consumption. Among other things, the practice of fasting or abstinence reminds us of the limitations of our body, and that includes our mortality. Feeling "stuffed" the day following Thanksgiving is but one indicator that we need to find healthier ways to consume food and drink.

The Wesleyan rule of life makes explicit the difference between worldly behaviors and practices and those actions that fit with being part of a "commonwealth of heaven" (Hebrews 12:1). In part because early Methodists were aware of the ways in which they were called to be "resident aliens" (1 Peter 2:11) in the world, they paid close attention to those "brothers" and "sisters" in Christ who, for one reason or another, were financially disadvantaged. In this respect, early Methodists were probably more conscious of class divisions than most Americans pretend to be today. Given the social structures of the suburban enclaves and "urban villas" in which many of us live, it is all too easy to arrange our lives so that we do not have to see social deprivation.

The phrase "laying up treasure upon earth" reflects the biblical imagery of Matthew's Gospel, which stands in contrast to the kind of trust displayed in the practice of fasting or abstinence. In addition to conveying a lack of trust in God, this image suggests the kind of greedy hoarding of possessions and/or wealth that does not fit with the distributive ethic of the Wesleyan rule of life. When we have confidence that God will provide, then we, like the ancient Israelites, will be content with our daily bread and display the confidence to avoid patterns of getting and spending that "lay waste our powers" (per Wordsworth) as children of the Heavenly King.

DAILY WORD

Do not store up for yourselves treasures on earth, where moth and rust consume and where thieves break in and steal; but store up for yourselves treasures in heaven, where neither moth nor rust consumes and where thieves do not break in and steal. For where your treasure is, there your heart will be also. (Matthew 6:19-20)

PRAYER

O God, help us to lay up treasures in heaven that our lives may reflect your holy love in the world and speak the coming of your rule in Christ. Amen.

SATURDAY: DAY TWENTY-ONE

RE-ENGAGING THE GENERAL RULES

United by God's grace, we commit ourselves to the way of discipleship (1) *by doing no harm, by avoiding evil of every kind, especially that which is most generally practiced,* such as **doing what we know is not for the glory of God, as: borrowing without probability of paying;** (2) *by doing good, as far as possible, to all men,* **by all possible diligence;** (3) by practicing the ordinary means of grace: **searching the Scriptures.**

Sometimes it is not enough to be diligent in "searching the Scriptures"; we still find ourselves deeply puzzled about what to do, and we have to linger with the uncertainties that plague our efforts to serve God in the world. Even then, we may be able to articulate for ourselves and others why a given course of action is imprudent, even if we find ourselves taking it—*at least for the time being.* When the average seminarian in 2010 has had to incur a debt of $40,000 for three years of theological training (not counting any indebtedness for undergraduate education) in order to prepare for service as a United Methodist minister, we cannot pretend that the problem has not been made clear to us! What we can do, however, is to agree to "bear with" one another in this circumstance, knowing that, in addition to the diligence we expect of one another in our individual roles, we must also find ways to work together to solve the problems that confront us.

We need not idealize early Methodism's virtuous behavior about money (the very reason the rules emerged was in response to problems that the early Methodists found themselves confronting in places like Bristol and London), nor can we ignore the ways United Methodist congregations and agencies have paid employees inadequately across the years. Nor do we need to succumb to the cynicism of believing that we do not have the power to do anything about our circumstance. Being diligent about paying our debts has a great deal to do with making it possible for one another to be diligent in the ministries that we undertake in common.

We cannot sustain excellence in ministry if the educational process that candidates go through means they are unable to be as diligent in their work because they are encumbered by debts they will be unlikely to have the ability to repay—regardless of how diligent they are.

As John Wesley made clear in his writings about "searching the scriptures," this practice of "reading in communion" was more of a common quest for wisdom than it was individuals seeking "proof-texts" to support their contentions. As we "watch over one another in love," we need to help one another cultivate *the courage to be puzzled* so that we can all take ownership of the problems and difficulties we face in our life together. Perhaps if we are diligent about facing the things that puzzle us the most, we will discover the wisdom that God will provide to help us resolve such conundrums.

DAILY WORD

But we appeal to you, brothers and sisters, to respect those who labor among you, and have charge of you in the Lord and admonish you; esteem them very highly in love because of their work. (1 Thess. 5:12-13)

PRAYER

O God, help us to bear with one another and to be patient with one another that our hope may remain in you and you alone. Amen.

PRAISING GOD WITH JOHN & CHARLES WESLEY

"Love Divine, All Loves Excelling" (No. 384 in *The United Methodist Hymnal*) has been a favorite hymn for many Christian congregations across the past three centuries.

Love divine, all loves excelling,
Joy of heaven, to earth come down;
Fix in us thy humble dwelling;
All they faithful mercies crown!
Jesus, thou art all compassion,
Pure, unbounded love thou art;
Visit us with thy salvation;
Enter every trembling heart.

Breathe, O breathe thy loving Spirit
Into every troubled breast!
Let us all in thee inherit;
Let us find that second rest.
Take away our bent to sinning;
Alpha and Omega be;
End of faith as its beginning,
Set our hearts at liberty.

Come, almighty to deliver,
Let us all thy life receive;
Suddenly return and never,
Nevermore thy temples leave.
Thee we would be always blessing,
Serve thee as thy hosts above,
Pray and praise thee without ceasing,
Glory in thy perfect love.

Finish then, thy new creation,
pure and spotless let us be,
Let us see thy great salvation
Perfectly restored in thee
Changed from glory into glory
Till in heaven we take our place,
Till we cast our crowns before thee.
Lost in wonder, love, and praise.

When we sing the words "set our hearts at liberty," among other things we are praying that God will not let us be consumed by self-interest. The fourth stanza of this wonderful hymn by Charles Wesley says it all! We envision the end of our days spent in glory "lost in wonder, love, and praise."

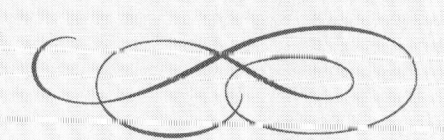

BELIEVE · LOVE · OBEY

WEEK FOUR

A Prayer for the Church in Mission

O God, as we continue in the path of discipleship may we recognize the love of your Son in our brothers and sisters in ministry.

May the rule of life that we have received through our own tradition inspire in us the desire to pass on this rule to others, that they will see the beauty of Christ in the mission of the church.

Gracious Lord, fill our hearts with gratitude and help us not to fall into despair.

Help us to see and to imagine your kingdom beyond the doors of our churches.

In our institutions of higher education . . .
In our institutions of health and welfare . . .
In our institutions for the elderly . . .
In our connectional roundtable and leadership table . . .
In our boards and agencies of our General Church . . .

Lord, help us to see that the work of Christ is bigger than any one piece and that the love of your Spirit breaks open the joy of service here and around the world.

May we all continue to be lost in the wonder and praise of our Savior Jesus Christ! Amen.

SUNDAY: DAY TWENTY-TWO

RE-ENGAGING THE GENERAL RULES

*We embody the Wesleyan way of salvation (1) by doing no harm, by avoiding evil of every kind, such as **profaning the day of the Lord by selling**; (2) by doing good; **for the Lord's sake**; (3) by attending upon all the ordinances of God: **the public worship of God**.*

As various Christian writers have observed across the centuries, Christian gatherings for public worship might be said to be rehearsals for the future enactment of our eternal worship of God. As Charles Wesley's hymn "Love Divine All Love's Excelling" displays so well, the Christian journey involves being *"Changed from glory to glory, Until in heaven we take our place, Till we cast our crowns before thee. Lost in wonder, love, and praise."* Wesley's understanding of the order of salvation did not stop with death, but imaged eternal life as continuing "glorification" (2 Cor. 3:18) as Christians continued their communion with God in a state of being "lost in wonder, love, and praise." From the perspective of John Wesley and the people called Methodists, this is the ultimate "calling" for Christians.

It follows, then, that our vision of our ultimate destiny before God also should govern all of our behaviors. With deliberate understatement, the "General Rules" stipulate that *all the good that we seek to do* should be "for the Lord's sake." While there are good reasons why various Methodists have hailed the "pragmatism" of John Wesley's approach to social endeavors, and he himself was fond of calling attention to the "good fruits" that would result from particular Christian practice, we should never forget that in the midst of the provisional judgments the founder of Methodism made, the ultimate criterion for doing good was "for the Lord's sake."

Once we have brought the criterion of doing good "for the Lord's sake" into perspective, then it is not difficult for contemporary United Methodists to grasp why they would not want to sell things on the day of the Lord. Engaging in commercial exchanges in which we profit is to forget what is ultimate, and thereby to profane sacred time set aside for worship and Sabbath rest. It can also be a misuse of the gifts of creation by refusing to acknowledge the extraordinary dispensation of God's grace, which cannot be purchased but is rather the free gift of God. At the same time, as we open our covenant circles to those who are seeking salvation, we will no doubt face the necessity of having to determine exceptions to the rule. By reminding ourselves that on those occasions when we might sell something that it would need to be "for the Lord's sake," we remind ourselves that our ultimate vocation will require us to know how to be "lost in wonder, love, and praise"—dispositions that are not enhanced by going to market on Sunday.

DAILY WORD

For we do not proclaim ourselves; we proclaim Jesus Christ as Lord and ourselves as your servants for Jesus' sake. For it is the God who said, 'Let light shine out of darkness,' who has shone in our hearts to give the light of the knowledge of the glory of God in the face of Jesus Christ. (2 Cor. 4:5-6)

PRAYER

For Christ's sake we offer our lives in praise, thanking him for his perfect sacrifice on the cross and for his eternal love in the kingdom. Amen.

MONDAY: DAY TWENTY-THREE

RE-ENGAGING THE GENERAL RULES

We embody the Wesleyan rule of life for spiritual formation (1) *by doing no harm, by avoiding evil of every kind, such as* **the singing those songs that do not tend to the knowledge or love of God**; (2) *by doing good*, **by running with patience**; (3) *by attending upon all the ordinances of God:* [**Christian conference or giving and receiving counsel**].

Throughout my spouse's ministry, I have had the privilege of sitting in the pew and "heartily" singing the great hymns of the church. One of the conversations that seems to replay over and over again in the congregations Mary has served is the debate about the proper role of music in the church. As a person who does not read music but who was raised in congregations that emphasized the importance of congregational singing and therefore knows a large number of hymns by heart, I enjoy offering my voice alongside that of others who are singing in unison. On one occasion, a choir director persisted despite my polite refusal to join the choir because she simply could not believe that I would value congregational singing over the importance of sustaining a strong choir of men and women.

The perennial conversation about the proper role of music in the church might be thought of as a good example of what it looks like to give and receive counsel about a matter that is central to the Christian life: praising God. A century ago, congregations split over whether to install organs, which provided a more euphonic "voice" in worship services, or to preserve the habits and practices of congregational singing, which of course is rather inconsistently euphonic in quality. I cannot imagine I would actually leave a congregation over this kind of disagreement, but I continue to place a high value on the importance of congregational singing, and whenever I can, I like to participate in hymn fests or "singings"—occasions where Christians gather to sing the great hymns of the Church.

Alas, not everyone shares my preferences in this matter! Part of the reason why the virtues of *patience* and *forbearance* are so important for a Wesleyan rule of life, then, is because we have to take seriously that the journey of Christian discipleship proceeds in the company of people with whom we may disagree about matters great and small. Because not everyone is capable of making the distinction between their personal preferences and "propriety," we are likely to find ourselves in situations where we have to talk through differences. Often, different generations in the church will disagree about which songs are appropriate in congregational gatherings for worship, and in some cases, such disagreements reflect judgments about the propriety of particular songs. (Is it appropriate for Joe to sing "Love is a Many Splendored Thing" at Jennifer's wedding? Should Red Smith's family be indulged in their desire to sing "Red Sails in the Sunset" after the benediction at his memorial service? Can the youth group sing "Amazing Grace" to the tune of "Gilligan's Island" or "House of the Rising Sun" on Sunday morning at the traditional worship service?)

Although the brothers Wesley could be priggish at times, we should remember that they also displayed a remarkable capability to draw on cultural forms to create hymns and songs of deep significance. Some of the tunes of Charles Wesley's most thoughtful hymns used popular tunes, showing that it is possible for music to result in greater knowledge and love of God.

DAILY WORD

But be filled with the Spirit, as you sing psalms and hymns and spiritual songs among yourselves, singing and making melody to the Lord in your hearts, giving thanks to God the Father at all times and for everything in the name of our Lord Jesus Christ. (Ephesians 5:18b-20)

PRAYER

Open my heart, O Lord, and let my lips declare your praises to all the earth. Amen.

TUESDAY: DAY TWENTY-FOUR

RE-ENGAGING THE GENERAL RULES

*It is therefore expected of all who continue in these societies that they should continue to evidence their desire for salvation; (1) by doing no harm, by avoiding evil of every kind, especially that which is most generally practiced, such as **reading those books which do not tend to the knowledge or love of God**; (2) by doing good; **by running the race which is set before them**; (3) by practicing the ordinary means of grace that God has given: **the ministry of the Word, either read or expounded**.*

I love to read books, and over the course of my lifetime I have been blessed to be able to read some extraordinarily rich and wonder-filled novels, poems, and essays, as well as nonfiction works ranging from historical monographs to philosophy and theology. Reading also was highly valued among the early Methodists—so much so, in fact, that time was taken to teach converts how to read so that they could actively participate in the ministry of the Word.[9]

In addition, in a set of books known as *The Christian Library*, Wesley identified what he regarded to be the 50 best examples of Christian writing from across the centuries. Nor did he ever shy away from commending contemporary writings such as William Law's *Serious Call to a Devout and Holy Life* to members of the Methodist societies.

Exercising discriminating judgment is not the same thing as exercising censorship. In fact, in a world flooded with the printed word and graphic images of all kinds, we find ourselves in greater need of wise counsel about what we should take the time to read and see. This is true for several reasons, but none more important than the simple fact that as disciples of Jesus Christ, we are following a "course of study" in which we are learning in what St. Benedict would have called "the school of Christ." Wesley thought it was very important for Methodists to be able to distinguish between "serious seeking" and the kind of aimless spiritual quest that refused to be disciplined.

Wesley and the people called Methodists would not have had many examples of novels in their time, but the notion that reading might be a form of entertainment that satisfied disordered desires was known to them. Pornography is but the most obvious example of "reading material" that is not conducive to knowing and loving God, but the prospect of *porneia* need not be the only reason to avoid a book or a film. We also want to be vigilant against things that distract us from discipleship.

As citizens of a culture that tends to elevate the authority of personal judgment over the collective wisdom of Christian tradition, some people bristle to hear that reading *The DaVinci Code* or the books in the *Left Behind* series is not helpful. The fact of the matter is that such counsel is true, particularly when they distract us from reading the Bible. Not to be able to make such distinctions is to render ourselves inarticulate about where we are going as disciples of Jesus Christ. Without the capacity to make discerning judgments, more likely than not we will fail to see the value of "the ministry of the Word, read or expounded."

DAILY WORD

Do nothing from selfish ambition or conceit, but in humility regard others as better than yourselves. Let each of you look not to your own interests, but to the interests of others. Let the same mind be in you that was in Christ Jesus. (Phil. 2:3-5)

PRAYER

O God, open our minds to your truth and fill our hearts with your love, that we may serve you in the power of your Holy Spirit in this world and the world to come. Amen.

WEDNESDAY: DAY TWENTY-FIVE

RE-ENGAGING THE GENERAL RULES

United by God's grace, we commit ourselves to the way of discipleship (1) *by doing no harm, by avoiding evil of every kind, especially that which is most generally practiced, such as* **softness and needless self-indulgence**; (2) *by doing good;* **denying themselves, and taking up their cross daily**; (3) *by attending upon all the ordinances of God:* **the Supper of the Lord.**

In the film *Romero*, the Archbishop of El Salvador is martyred while celebrating the Eucharist at the Cathedral in San Salvador. In this dramatic and moving scene, Oscar Romero, played by the actor Raul Julia, is killed by those who oppose his solidarity with the poor of the country of El Salvador. American audiences of this film are sometimes shocked by the ways in which the priestly action of presiding at the Eucharist turns out to be rendered quite literally as Romero's martyrdom is enacted in the context of the paschal mystery of dying with Jesus Christ, who offered himself as a living sacrifice.

The stern language of the rules for avoiding evil and doing good for this day seems to require some translation in an era when therapeutic idioms seem to dominate our culture, resulting in a wide variety of practices of "self-care" and personal well-being. As the author of a book entitled *The Primitive Physic*, John Wesley was hardly insensible to the need for caring for one's health, but neither did he subscribe to a utopian definition of "health" in which virtually anything can be justified if one wants it badly enough. Seeking a disciplined middle ground, Wesley advocated getting exercise and eating carefully and well. At the same time, he was quite serious about preparing Methodists for the prospect that they could be persecuted, and in extreme cases perhaps even martyred. For that reason, Methodists should avoid those common behaviors of "needless self-indulgence." The operative word here is "needless."

For Wesley, needless self-indulgence constituted those behaviors that would lead Methodists to be unprepared for the opportunity to offering "living witness" (in life or in death) to the good news about the life, death, ministry, and resurrection of Jesus of Nazareth. Here we have to make careful distinctions between "want" and "need," taking into account not only our desires but also the needs and desires of those around us. We also need to recover the early Methodist awareness of the possibility of martyrdom. In truth, United Methodists have not had many occasions to develop or transmit wisdom about martyrdom in recent years, but that does not mean that we will not face such challenges in the coming years. Regardless, we must learn to recognize the ways in which, each day, we are called to die and be raised with Christ. The Eucharist that we celebrate with other Christians when we gather as the church should shape the life that we live each day.

DAILY WORD

Whoever does not carry the cross and follow me cannot be my disciple. (Luke 14:27)

PRAYER

By the power of your love on the cross, dear Lord, convict us of our self-righteousness and forgive us our sins, that the good we do is in keeping with your transforming grace. Amen.

THURSDAY: DAY TWENTY-SIX

RE-ENGAGING THE GENERAL RULES

It is therefore expected of all who continue in these societies that they should continue to evidence their desire for salvation (1) by doing no harm, by avoiding evil of every kind, especially that which is most generally practiced, such as **laying up treasure upon earth**; *(2) by doing good . . .* **submitting to bear the reproach of Christ**; *(3) by attending upon all the ordinances of God:* **family and private prayer.**

The brothers Wesley were committed to the "stewardship" of holy things in a world in which the industrial revolution was wreaking havoc on the lives of ordinary men, women, and children. On the one hand, John and Charles Wesley wanted to bring the good news of the gospel to all the citizens of England as well as throughout the world. They also wanted the people of England to be able to live in conditions that made it possible for them to participate in the ancient Christian patterns of daily prayer that Wesley associated with the best features of ancient Christian tradition. To accomplish these purposes often involved speaking truth to power in ways that evoked negative responses from the "principalities and powers"—including those in the established church who did not think Wesley's ministry was "proper" or duly authorized.

What those religious and secular authorities may not have appreciated was the fact that John Wesley shared many of their instincts. After all he was an Oxford don, and he was accustomed to preaching in universities, cathedrals, and parish churches. He was not eager to venture outside the precincts of the Church of England to carry out his ministry. As he became convinced that God was calling him to engage in "field preaching" as a way of reaching out to coal miners and others, he noted in his journal that he had "submitted to be vile." In these same contexts, he also used the phrase "submitting to bear the reproach of Christ" to remind himself and fellow "Methodists" that they could expect to be rejected as part of their own participation in the paschal mystery. Just as Jesus was rejected by members of his hometown synagogue (Luke 4:14-30), so also Methodists could expect to be opposed in their efforts to "spread scriptural holiness across the land, reforming the continent, beginning with the church."

This is yet another example of the fluid way in which the Wesleys drew upon their extensive knowledge of the Scriptures of the Old and New Testaments to provide guidance to members of the "united societies" in early Methodism. Rather than spending their time "laying up treasures on earth," John and Charles Wesley drew upon the riches of the Christian tradition to write hymns and sermons and to edit texts from earlier segments of Christian tradition, as well as to call attention to contemporary resources (books, pamphlets, hymns, songs, and prayers) that could sustain "true Christianity." In that respect, they can be said to be like the "scribes of the kingdom" that Jesus described in Matthew 13:52. They had the discerning ability to know how to bring forth treasures old and new from the storehouse. However, John and Charles Wesley wanted all Methodists to have the opportunity to exercise the stewardship of the Kingdom of God, a "calling" for which the practice of family and private prayer served as a necessary first step in Wesley's version of the "school of the Lord's service."

DAILY WORD

"Have you understood all this?" They answered, "Yes." And he said to them, "Therefore every scribe who has been trained for the kingdom of heaven is like the master of a household who brings out of his treasure what is new and what is old." (Matthew 13:51-52)

PRAYER

O Lord, help us as servants in your church to bring forth treasures old and new that, empowered by your Holy Spirit, we may discern the renewing direction of your love. Amen.

FRIDAY: DAY TWENTY-SEVEN

RE-ENGAGING THE GENERAL RULES

It is therefore expected of all who continue in these societies that they should continue to evidence their desire for salvation; (1) by doing no harm, by avoiding evil of every kind, such as **buying men, women, and children with an intention to enslave them**; *(2) by doing good,* **to be as the filth and offscouring of the world**; *(3) by attending upon all the ordinances of God:* **fasting or abstinence.**

Not many contemporary United Methodists living in the USA find ourselves in danger of being regarded as "the filth and offscouring of the world"—a phrase that probably seems rather oddly pious and old-fashioned to people who live comfortable lives in towns and cities where most of us are regarded as good citizens with reputations for leadership in church and community. During Wesley's lifetime, however, Methodists struggled against various forms of social disapproval, including that of fellow members of the Church of England who suspected them of being "dissenters," a charge that would be expressed in various ways and at times would even take on exotic forms, such as the accusation that John Wesley was actually a Jesuit or a Dominican in disguise.

In such a circumstance, fasting or abstinence from food and drink at particular times* was a way for disciplined men and women to keep "spiritually fit" for the challenges of living in a world in which, to live your life according to a rule of life for spiritual formation, was to risk being verbally abused—or in some instances to suffer physical abuse by mobs seeking a scapegoat for local social problems. Although Wesley did not focus a lot of his writings on fasting as a mode of individual and corporate repentance, he clearly believed that this was a proper use of this particular means of grace. In another sense, Wesley contended that Methodists should not object unduly to the ways worldly neighbors regarded them. To be "as the filth and offscouring of the world" could have been a reminder also of the need to be in solidarity with those who were oppressed, including those who were enslaved and subject to the indignities of racist claims of white superiority.

Although Wesley did not live to see the "shipwreck" of the people called Methodists that occurred in the mid-nineteenth century in the United States over the issue of slavery, he was well aware of the fact that listing the "buying . . . of men, women, and children with the intention to enslave them" served as a marker that limited Methodist commercial exchange in a variety of ways. As we cast a glance back over more than two centuries of schism that resulted from Methodist recalcitrance over the issue of slavery and more generally a host of more minor disagreements about how to practice the General Rules, perhaps contemporary United Methodists should consider fasting as an act of repentance for the ways that we and our forebears have failed to display the integrity of the Wesleyan rule of life.

*Please note: Wesley advocated keeping the traditional Anglican fast, which lasted from Thursday evening until Friday afternoon at 3 p.m.

DAILY WORD

"Teacher, which commandment in the law is the greatest?" He said to them, 'You shall love the Lord your God with all your heart, and with all your soul, and with all your mind.' This is the greatest and first commandment. And a second is like it: 'You shall love your neighbor as yourself.' (Matthew 22:36-39)

PRAYER

Living God, unite our hearts and minds and souls toward the common mission we have in Christ, that we may be spiritually fit for the work to which you have called us and sent us. Amen.

SATURDAY: DAY TWENTY-EIGHT

RE-ENGAGING THE GENERAL RULES

It is therefore expected of all who continue therein that they should continue to evidence their desire for salvation (1) by doing no harm, by avoiding evil of every kind, such as **the buying or selling of of men, women, and children with an intention to enslave them**; *(2) by doing good;* [anticipating the likelihood] *that men should say all manner of evil of them falsely, for the Lord's sake*; *(3) by practicing the means of grace that God has given:* **searching the Scriptures.**

One reason why we should immerse ourselves in the world of Christian scripture is that a lifetime of living with biblical writings will equip us with a storehouse of images and narratives that we can use to gain perspective as we encounter problems on our journey of faith. Some years ago, a colleague told me that he had overheard a conversation in which someone on our campus called me "the Osama Bin Laden of the university." I was initially stunned, but then I found myself laughing at the extravagant nature of this insult.

One of the reasons I was able to ignore the insult was because I understood that at that moment I was living in an institutional environment dominated by America's "culture wars." As someone who prefers not to think of himself as conforming to either a "fundamentalist" (right wing) agenda or a "progressive" (left wing) orientation, I recognize that almost any initiative in spiritual and religious matters was likely to be interpreted according to that grid. In this case, a member of the "progressive" party on campus mistook me for a fundamentalist. On other occasions, members of the "fundamentalist" party at our university have attributed evil motives and aspirations to me in ways equally unfounded.

In the midst of such conflicted circumstances (which are by no means confined to academic settings), it is important for us to be able to locate sources of stability. When vilified by others, I have sometimes re-read the stories of Joseph and Daniel to remind myself what it means to persevere in the midst of unjust accusations. Over the course of our lifetime, "searching the Scriptures" is the practice of Christian discipleship that helps to sustain us in the midst of shifting scenes of conflict and suspicion. Like a trellis that keeps a fragile plant oriented to the sun, the practice of searching the scriptures helps to keep us oriented toward those sources of illumination that can "steer the pilgrim's course aright."

As anyone familiar with the history of American Methodism knows, over the course of the nineteenth century, the integrity of the General Rules became subject to a variety of internal and external challenges, and despite commentary after commentary, this "discipline within the Discipline" became more of a relic than a functioning part of a trellis for spiritual formation. The dilemma of Bishop James O. Andrew, who inherited slaves from his dead wife's estate that by law he could not release from slavery, proved to be the issue around which the division of Methodism into Northern and Southern "churches" occurred. Although today Methodism in the American context is "United," in many precincts it feels "untied" instead, and Methodism is sometimes mocked. At the same time, it remains possible to turn insults into badges of honor as together we embody a rule of life for spiritual formation.

DAILY WORD

There is no fear in love, but perfect love casts out fear; for fear has to do with punishment, and whoever fears has not reached perfection in love. We love because he first loved us. (1 John 4:18-19)

PRAYER

O Lord, may you perfect us in your love, that as your church we may grow unto the likeness of your Son in the power of your Holy Spirit. Praise be to God! Amen.

PRAISING GOD WITH JOHN & CHARLES WESLEY

"Come On, My Partners in Distress" (#324 in *Collected Works of John Wesley, Vol. 13*) is a hymn that I imagine members of Methodist bands and classes once sang to encourage one another not to give in to the temptation to let earthly obstacles prevent them from keeping their eyes fixed on kingdom purposes. With the "gospel ordinances" as aids for staying on track, it is indeed possible to look past present conflicts to a future of communion with the Triune God made possible by Jesus Christ our Savior.

Come on, my partners in distress,
My comrades through the wilderness,
Who still your bodies feel;
Awhile forget your griefs and fears
And look beyond this vale of tears
To that celestial hill.

Beyond the bounds of time and space,
Look forward to that heavenly place,
The saints' secure abode;
On faith's strong eagle pinions rise,
And force your passage to the skies,
And scale the mount of God.

Who suffer with our Master here,
We shall before his face appear,
And by his side sit down;
To patient faith the prize is sure,
And all that to the end endure
The cross, shall wear the crown.

Thrice blessed bliss-inspiring hope!
It lifts the fainting spirits up,
It brings to life the dead;
Our conflicts here shall soon be past,
And you and I ascend at last
Triumphant with our Head.

The promise that we will "ascend at last" as part of the triumph of Jesus Christ should encourage us to put away petty squabbles in favor of working together for the sake of the church's mission. Early Methodists knew firsthand that whether they were able to "maintain the unity of the spirit in the bonds of peace" (Ephesians 4:4) had an effect on their evangelistic efforts. In fact, for more than a century, Methodist disciplines included a section "On the Necessity of Union with One Another." Perhaps we need to restore that kind of humble resolve to seek unity in future editions of the United Methodist *Book of Discipline*. In the meantime, we work together in our common mission of making disciples of Jesus Christ with "patient faith," because we know that "the prize is sure."

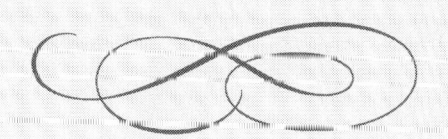

AFTERWORD: LEARNING TO KEEP THE CIRCLE OPEN

"These are the General Rules of our societies; all of which we are taught of God to observe, even in his written Word, which is the only rule, and the sufficient rule, both of our faith and practice. And all these we know his Spirit writes on truly awakened hearts. . . ."[10]

The covenant group that I have been part of for the past decade gathers on Monday mornings at a United Methodist church on the edge of the city of Indianapolis. Over the years, the three of us have learned how to engage one another amid the ups and downs of our respective spiritual journeys and ministerial callings. Whenever I am trying to describe to someone how a covenant group can provide support for Christian discipleship, I recall an incident that took place about seven years ago.

After my friends Glen and Marie shared their prayer concerns and sought counsel about concerns in their lives, I briefly told them that I had been invited to pursue a professional opportunity at another church-related university. I mentioned several family concerns that made me hesitant to permit my name to go forward in the search process, and I also talked about some of the ways that I was attracted to that kind of opportunity. At several points Glen and Marie asked questions to clarify what I was saying.

At one point, Glen asked me a probing question. "Michael, are you willing to be obedient to God's call in your life?" After thinking about it for a moment, I replied with a rueful grin, "Glen, to tell you the truth, I really don't want to have to think about God's will at this point in my journey. So I guess the answer to your question is, 'No.'" At that particular moment, it seemed as if I was not living up to the covenant of Christian discipleship.

But of course, that is not the whole story. The snapshot that I have provided of my covenant group captures a single moment in a conversation that has now been going on for more than ten years at the beginning of each week. Marie and Glen know me well enough to know I would have to live with the words I had spoken. They knew that my apparent refusal to discern about how God was calling me did not convey my deepest longings or highest hopes as an ordained minister. They also knew that at least some of what I had said was colored by my overall sense of fatigue after several months of intensive work as well as a lingering sense of discouragement.

Our covenant group that morning concluded with a prayer offered by Glen. In addition to offering petitions for all of us, Glen prayed that God would grant me rest and restore a sense of perspective. Several months later, I revisited this matter with the group. By that time I had found a way to resume discerning about God's call in my life. While I still had reservations about the prospect of considering a move to another city, I had rejoined the conversation of the "open circle" defined by the covenant of obedience that I share with these colleagues in ministry.

Sharing the Yoke of Obedience: Remembering the Early Methodist Spiritual Ethos

Previous generations of Methodist laity and clergy found it meaningful to talk about how they shared the "yoke of obedience." This image, which has been taken from the "Wesley Covenant Prayer," has its origins in the kind of agrarian context in which oxen were paired together in service to a farmer. The Wesleyan usage builds on the biblical background that partially inspired John Wesley and the people called Methodists. Most 21st-century spiritual pilgrims no longer resonate with such images, in part because we do not encounter the practice of being "yoked together" in daily life.

Perhaps in the coming years, United Methodist clergy and laity will discover a new set of ordinary images that we can use to describe the ways in which we experience Christian conference as a means of grace. In the meantime, I hope we continue to choose to "deliver our souls" to one another in the context of covenant discipleship groups and other forms of Christian conference in which "brothers" and "sisters" in Christ dare to watch over one another in love, refusing to permit one another to indulge in self-deception and thereby displaying more insights than what therapeutic techniques can provide.

I would like to think that this commentary on the General Rules contains material that would be helpful to people who are involved in covenant groups like the one I have described here. Nothing in this set of commentaries should be taken to mean that Wesleyan spirituality can be undertaken as an individual endeavor. However deeply personal "seeking God" may be, it is never defined solely by the individual's perspective or changing sensibilities.

For Wesley and the people called Methodists, the Wesleyan rule of life was an ordered quest that made sense in the context of an "open circle" of Christians "watching over one another in love" in the context of covenanted commitments to live according to a rule of life. For that reason, as Lester Ruth has pointed out, "The most succinct summary of the early Methodist ethos is the document that John Wesley crafted at the beginning of the movement—the 'General Rules.'"[11]

"Deep desire and longing were central to early Methodist spirituality. The affective dimension of their lives was fully engaged, but not in a way that undercut the ethical dimension. Desire, whether to avoid the coming wrath of God or to seek the eternal enjoyment of God, was to be demonstrated in a certain way of living. Love for God, for instance, was expected to result in abhorrence of the 'vice of criminal amusement in the world' on the one hand and in a grasping of righteousness on the other. While early Methodists expressed much of their ethos as the avoidance of certain behaviors, avoiding evil was only part of the story. The goal was not just to avoid hell, it was to be made fit to enjoy the God of heaven. This meant the reshaping of lives."[12]

As Lester Ruth goes on to make very clear, "This ethos was not just a matter of individual behavior."

"The Methodist vision was for a holy *people*. This communal vision stood behind the rigorous Methodist ethos. Methodists assumed their distinctive way of life as part of their communal identity, particularly as it marked them as different from the surrounding culture. There was no witness—and no path to heaven—in conformity. Individual Methodists identified with the group by accepting this communal ethos and desiring to live by it. The ethos provided a boundary that marked the group, distinguishing it from the surrounding culture."[13]

And we dare not forget that the means of grace that were used in that ordered quest also were provisional in character. They had to be in order to engage the challenges of a world being dramatically altered by the machinery of the Industrial Revolution in England. Throughout their lives, John and Charles Wesley practiced self-examination in different ways. For example, during their Oxford years, John and Charles attempted to have their actions "guided by lists of questions for self-examination that were arranged according to the virtues for each day of the week: love of God, love of neighbor, humility, mortification and self-denial, resignation, and meekness, and thanksgiving. The 'one thing needful' was a soul renewed in the image of God."[14]

Although John Wesley provided a wealth of written texts that he believed could provide inspiration and enrichment for the serious seekers of his day, it is worth noting that he did not attempt to provide early Methodists with a text that pretended to be a comprehensive guide to Christian spirituality. In its own way, then, the Wesleyan "rule of life"—like the *Rule of St. Benedict*—can be said to be "a rule for beginners." And it is also a rule of life for people who find that they need to begin again. While the Wesleyan way rightly aspires to Christian perfection, it is a mistake to think of spiritual formation as an all or nothing matter.

The Wesleyan Rule of Life, then, is a modest structure. Like a trellis that enables a plant to grow and thrive by providing support, the practices associated with the "General Rules" provide *just enough structure* for those who are committed to live a covenantal life to be able to grow in healthy ways, and *just enough freedom* to be able to explore in a wise manner, provided that those who share its provisions have covenanted with one another in a robust way.

Renew Our Covenant: Watching Over One Another in Love

Over the years that I have been writing and teaching about the General Rules of the United Societies, I have developed a strong conviction that any reading of the General Rules that ignores the role played by the practice of the annual "covenant renewal" is incomplete and misleading. Like the "gospel ordinances," the practice of covenant renewal is integral to our intention to live according to a Wesleyan rule of life for spiritual formation. And I also believe that it is one of the practices that is most crucial for us to reclaim for the sake of carrying out our mission of making disciples of Jesus Christ for the transformation of the world.

The so-called Wesleyan Covenant Prayer is not one of John Wesley's original contributions but is a remarkable prayer nonetheless, as countless Methodists and others who have claimed the spiritual heritage across the past three centuries have discovered for themselves. As Keith Beasley Topliffe has shown us, there is great wisdom to be gleaned from this classic prayer.

> I am no longer my own, but thine.
> Put me to what thou wilt,
> rank me with whom thou wilt;
> put me to doing, put me to suffering,
> let me be employed for thee, or laid aside for thee,
> exalted for thee, or brought low for thee;
> let me be full, let me be empty;

let me have all things, let me have nothing.
I freely and heartily yield all things
to thy pleasure and disposal.
And now, O glorious and blessed God,
Father, Son and Holy Spirit
Thou art mine, and I am thine. So be it.
And the covenant which I have made on earth,
let it be ratified in heaven. Amen [15]

Not everyone would want to pray this prayer, and certainly there are days when some of us find its lovely poetic words to be daunting and even intimidating. As my own response to the probing question of my good friend Glen indicates (see above), there are days when—if we are going to be honest with one another—we do not want to surrender our wills to God's purposes in the world. It is one thing for that to happen on a given day. It is quite another circumstance, when a man or woman comes to the point of saying that they no longer wish to be accountable to those with whom they share the "yoke of obedience" in the ways that they have covenanted to be accountable.

Being Sustained by (and Sustaining) the Open Circle of Covenant Community

"If there be any among us who observe them not, who habitually break any of them, let it be known unto them who watch over that soul as they who must give an account. We will admonish him of the error of his ways. We will bear with him for a season. But then, if he repent not, he hath no more place among us. We have delivered our own souls."[16]

Some contemporary readers may find the final sentences of the "General Rules of the United Societies" to be troubling, since those words candidly image the prospect of a covenant community breaking fellowship with someone who no longer wants to seek God. In a culture marked by unchecked individualism, such "disciplined candor" can be mistaken for inhospitable behavior, but it is best described as "speaking the truth in love." Communities of faith that live according to a "rule of life" must be disciplined enough to be able to welcome those who want to be serious seekers. They are also communities that care enough to be able to tell a brother or sister in Christ when he or she no longer is grounded in the spirit of repentance. They should also be the kinds of communities of faith in which the effects of "speaking the truth in love" are experienced as "good fruit."

In sum: if we are going to be able to reclaim the Wesleyan Rule of Life for the church's mission, United Methodists and others who claim the Wesleyan heritage must learn the art of sustaining an "open circle." And this is where the simplicity of loving obedience and mutual accountability (see "Believe. Love. Obey" above) seems to run into difficulty. As we all learned in our "basic geometry" course, circles are by their definition closed figures—within a two-dimensional plane.

Nonetheless, what may not be possible, strictly speaking, in the study of geometry *can be said to be true* in the economy of God's grace, where human action is enabled by the gracious winds of the Holy Spirit. The covenant established in relation to the General Rules provides the focus to enable the formation of the circle, and the practice of Christian hospitality pushes those in the circle to be open to reforming the circle in different ways, including forming new circles (each defined by the common covenant). The Wesleyan "rule of life" for spiritual formation, then, is the kind of "trellis" that is sustained in community.

Even with such clarifications in view, we know it is not easy to maintain the "open circle." Controversies will arise whether or not we bother to sing or pray Charles Wesley's poignant hymn "Come On, My Partners in Distress" (p. 53). In the 19th century Methodists struggled to sustain their version of the open circle in the midst of disagreements about how to deal with the moral issue of slavery. In our own time, United Methodists are divided about how to think about the ordination of gays and lesbians as well as other issues. There probably has never been a time when the prospect of division was not a challenge for some branch of the Wesleyan family.

I often wonder, though, whether the "culture wars" would be so easily perpetuated in the UMC if more clergy and more laity decided to be intentional about participating in covenant groups. When we allow ourselves to be reshaped (by God's grace) to be able to support one another's struggles to live out the covenant, and where we are able (by God's grace) to be hospitable to conversations about topics that make us all uncomfortable, the open circle becomes possible in time and space. Much of the time, it seems to me, the only kinds of conversations that are taking place are those constituted by "closed circles" of *ungenerous orthodoxy* and *condescending progressivism*. Neither side really seems to own up to the brokenness of the "body" of faith, much less express hope about the capacity for healing and reconciliation.

Sustaining Hope for One Another in Reclaiming the Mission of the Church

Amid all those things that we find distracting, we need to find ways to remind one another that we are called to be a people of hope. This reminds me of a memorable exchange that occurred years ago during an annual conference in another jurisdiction.

The Executive Committee of the Board of Ministry was making its report to the Executive Session of the ordained clergy members of the conference. At one point, the person delivering the report listed the name of a colleague who had turned in his orders in the face of having been charged with a disciplinary offense. This information was received in stunned silence. Events had unfolded so recently that virtually no one in the hall had an idea about the circumstances, and many sat staring at one another in bafflement.

Then, from the back of the hall, a hand went up. The person stood and asked a question: "Can you tell us anything about the nature of this matter?" The person reporting on behalf of the board consulted with his committee members before returning to the podium, and inquired: "For what purpose will the information be used?" The pastor replied: "I need to know in order to know how to pray for our brother in Christ that he may be restored to this fellowship of clergy." I vividly recall feeling convicted by the "right-headed" character of this response. Where others in the company of covenanted clergy may have been tempted to speculate about the reasons why this member of the conference had turned in his credentials, the person who asked the question kept his eyes on the prospect of restoration of the wayward brother.

A few years later, in another annual conference, I was present when a minister who had been disciplined many years before was received back into the fellowship of the clergy at the clergy executive session. I recall hearing this person acknowledge before those gathered that his "journey back" had been a long one, but that he was grateful to be able to serve once again. Unfortunately, there are United Methodist clergy and laity who have no practical experience of such restoration. This is but another reason why it is important for United Methodist clergy and laity alike to commit ourselves to participate in covenant groups where we can see for ourselves what it means for brothers and sisters to bear with us in the midst of our respective efforts to "work out our salvation with fear and trembling."

Those who would dare to be "serious seekers," who dare to covenant with others "to watch over one another in love," cannot afford to engage in wishful thinking that living according to a Wesleyan "rule of life" will spare us having to experience the brokenness of human relationships or the fragmentation that results from hidden sin. Nor should we allow ourselves to succumb to the cynicism that would presume that it is impossible for relationships to be healed and fellowship to be restored. *We can dare to be optimistic* about the prospects for reconciliation when fellowship is broken because of the superabundance of God's grace, and we can testify to the possibility of forgiveness because we know that each one of us has been forgiven.

That does not mean, however, that we are ever going to be in a position to control the course or duration of our journey of faith. Like members of a ship's crew, we are not in a position to determine our fate. We do not control when and where the wind of the Spirit will blow, or where we will find ourselves appointed in service to the church. What we can do is to be ready to practice the skills and disciplines that are grounded in the ordinary means of grace, and let those "gospel ordinances" orient us as we encounter the various challenges and opportunities that each day brings us, whether it is a day that we spend with fellow Christian brothers and sisters or one that we spend with the strangers (including non-Christians) with whom we may find ourselves at particular moments.

As those clergy and laity who have learned to love Charles Wesley's hymns discover sooner or later, scriptural allusions are so pervasive that it is not possible to identify all of those he may have had in mind when he wrote particular hymns. With that in mind, I have sometimes wondered if Charles Wesley had the story of what happened to St. Paul and others on board the ship during the storm in mind as he wrote the hymn that is so closely associated with the General Rules of the United Societies (see Appendix B). Even if that idea was not his specific intention, I think Acts 27:1-44 is a good passage to bring into view as we think about our individual lives as well as our participation in the United Methodist congregations in which we live out our discipleship "before the eyes of the watching world."

As John Wesley continually tried to show the people called Methodists, there is much wisdom to be gleaned from such passages of scripture about the self-styled "ambassador for Jesus Christ" (2 Corinthians 5). Some recent commentators have highlighted the paradox displayed in this story. As a prisoner of the Roman Empire, Paul is still able to exercise remarkable freedom in the context of carrying out his mission. In doing so, he did not allow his status as a prisoner of the state to determine the limits of his mission for Christ. He continued to point others to the kingdom of God while sharing his giftedness in ways that disconcerted those around him.[17]

This biblical example displays the kind of spiritual imagination displayed by the clergy and laity associated with early Methodism. Over and over again, John Wesley and the people called Methodists stated their collective mission as a "called out" company of men and women to "spread scriptural holiness across the land and reform the continent beginning with the church." As several cultural observers and more than a few United Methodist theologians have noted, the United Methodist Church in the first decade of the 21st century stands in much the same position as did the Church of England in Wesley's day. It remains to be seen whether the strategies that 18th-century advocates of "renewing the church" by practicing "true Christianity" can be successfully deployed in our time, but I for one believe that our tradition retains resources from which we can gain insight as we try to engage the daunting challenges of our own time.

And, like John Wesley and the earliest generation of Methodists, we can praise God for those "gospel ordinances" that we have been given to "steer [our] course aright" and ultimately "lead us to eternal day." As persons who have been schooled in the Wesleyan heritage of covenant discipleship, we can "watch over one another in love" with the humility of knowing that any of us may transgress. At the same time, we believe we should do so with the confidence that should any one of us "fall" during the course of our lives, even with those with whom we share the covenant, we will care enough to reach out, that we will have the opportunity to begin anew.

Concluding Reflections: Practicing Gratitude

Just as each day provides us with the opportunity to recognize that God has brought about a new beginning in human history as well as in our lives, each night provides us with the opportunity to rest in the assurance that nothing can separate us from the love of God in Christ Jesus. In this respect, I have come to cherish the "songs" of Zechariah, Mary, and Simeon from Luke's Gospel as markers that remind me throughout the day that *God's grace is sufficient for the day* in a world where God has revealed himself to us in the life, death, ministry, and resurrection of Jesus Christ.

I am also grateful for the persons in the covenant groups in which I have participated over the years (clergy and laity alike). These friends in Christ have offered their insights about the means of grace to help steer me back into the fold, where I can resume my place as one who shares in the "yoke of obedience." In that respect, I believe that we need to take more seriously the possibility that God can use our modest attempts to "watch over one another in love" than we are sometimes tempted to do. Only then can we begin to locate where we are as we experience the paschal mystery in the daily, weekly, monthly, and annual cycles of our existence.

Finally, we need to remind one another to be grateful for the spiritual resources that we have inherited. Along with the Historical Questions that ordinands are asked to address and Articles of Religion and the EUB Confession of Faith, the General Rules and the "Wesley Covenant Renewal Service" are treasures of our church. We should never take for granted that these sources of Christian wisdom are part of what makes it possible for us to watch over one another in love. In the meantime, we wait with hope for the day when all of God's people share old Simeon's song:

> "Lord, now you let your servant depart in peace;
> Your word has been fulfilled . . ."

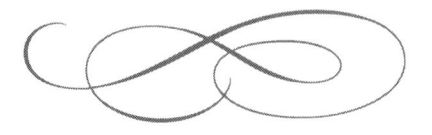

ACKNOWLEDGMENTS

I first began thinking about writing a devotional commentary on "The General Rules of the United Societies" while doing research for an article that was later published in *Asbury Theological Journal* in 1992. Since then, I have had occasion to write other articles, such as "The General Rules Revisited" (1999), and I have led numerous retreats for UM clergy and laity in which I have invited United Methodists to engage in conversations about this very significant document that lies at the heart of our church's tradition.

My reflections on this occasion also are informed by my own participation in covenant groups in various precincts over the past two decades. It is difficult to name all of the ways that Rev. Marie Lang & Rev. Glen Bell (in Indiana) and Rev. Aimee Twigg & Rev. Monte Holland (in Pennsylvania) have nurtured my faith as a Christian disciple over the past 22 years, but I am glad to have this occasion to say thanks to them for their encouragement, hospitality, and forbearance. In a different but no less important respect, my wife the Rev. Mary Wilder Cartwright (also a member of the Indiana Conference UMC) also has encouraged me in my journey of faith before and after we were ordained together. And I thank all of the other "brothers" and "sisters" in Christ that I have encountered along the way for their patience across the years. Truly they have watched over me in love.

In thinking about the General Rules, I have benefited from conversations with the wider Christian community. I also have benefited from my conversations with various Benedictine monastic men and women, especially my former UIndy colleague, Sr. Jennifer Horner of Our Lady of Grace Monastery, Fr. Noah Casey, a monk of St. Meinrad's Archabbey, and Abbot Timothy Kelly of St. John's Abbey in Collegeville, Minn. In particular, I am grateful to Mary Ewing Stamps and others who participated in the St. Brigid of Kildare Methodist-Benedictine Consultation (2002–04).

That consultation provided the occasion for me to think through the ways in which the General Rules constitute a rule of life for spiritual formation.

A fourth group of persons who contributed to this have been selected clergy in the Indiana Area of the United Methodist Church. It would not have been possible to complete this resource without the feedback that I received from a group of clergy in the South Indiana Conference of the United Methodist Church. In December 2005, I distributed copies of a draft of this resource to members of the Residents-in-Ministry (RIM) group of the South Indiana Conference of the United Methodist Church. When I met with that group in January 2006, we discussed their experience of attempting to use it. Based on this feedback, I revised the resource. Although I had already planned to incorporate passages of scripture and a daily prayer, the participants in the RIM group confirmed my sense that these would be essential additions. I am grateful to Andy Kinsey, the Wesleyan Theologian for the Indiana Conference UMC and Dean of the Wesleyan Connexion Project, for taking the time to add these features to the text. Without his collaboration, it would have been even more difficult to find the time to complete this resource.

Finally, I am also grateful for comments and criticism that I have received along with the words of encouragement from Ron Anderson, Kenneth Carter, Jr., Darren Cushman-Wood, Jerry Haas, Greg Jones, Andy Kinsey, Brent Laytham, Steve Long, Steve Manskar, and various other people have shown in this project across the years. Once again, Jeannine Allen has designed a wonderful layout. Lois Stead and Joey Beutel proofread an earlier version of this text. Cindy Tyree and Peter Noot have proofread the most recent set of revisions. I am grateful for the errors they have caught. Any remaining errors are my responsibility.

—*Michael Cartwright, Advent, 2010*

APPENDIX A: THE GENERAL RULES OF THE UNITED SOCIETIES (LONDON, 1743)

There is only one condition . . . required of those who desire admission into these societies: "a desire to flee from the wrath to come, and to be saved from their sins." But wherever this is really fixed in the soul it will be shown by its fruits.

It is therefore expected of all who continue therein that they should continue to evidence their desire for salvation.

FIRST: By doing no harm, by avoiding evil of every kind, especially that which is most generally practiced, such as

a) The taking of the name of God in vain.

b) The profaning the day of the Lord, either by doing ordinary work therein or by buying or selling.

c) Drunkenness: buying or selling spirituous liquors, or drinking them, unless in cases of extreme necessity.

d) The buying or selling of men, women, and children with an intention to enslave them.

e) Fighting, quarreling, brawling, brother going to law with brother; returning evil for evil, or railing for railing; the using many words in buying or selling.

f) The buying or selling goods that have not paid the duty.

g) The giving or taking things on usury—i.e., unlawful interest.

h) Uncharitable or unprofitable conversation; particularly speaking evil of magistrates or of ministers.

i) Doing to others as we would not they should do unto us.

j) Doing what we know is not for the glory of God, as:

    1. The putting on of gold and costly apparel.

    2. The taking such diversions as cannot be used in the name of the Lord Jesus.

    3. The singing those songs, or reading those books, which do not tend to the knowledge or love of God.

    4. Softness and needless self-indulgence.

    5. Laying up treasure upon earth.

    6. Borrowing without probability of paying; or taking up goods without a probability of paying for them.

It is expected of all who continue in these societies that they should continue to evidence their desire of salvation.

SECONDLY: By doing good; by being in every kind merciful after their power; as they have opportunity, doing good of every possible sort, and, as far as possible, to all men:

a) To their bodies, of the ability which God giveth, by giving food to the hungry, by clothing the naked, by visiting or helping them that are sick or in prison.

b) To their souls, by instructing, reproving, or exhorting all we have any intercourse with; trampling under foot that enthusiastic doctrine that "we are not to do good unless *our hearts be free to it.*"

c) By doing good, especially to them that are of the household of faith or groaning so to be; employing them preferably to others; buying one of another, helping each other in business, and so much the more because the world will love its own and them only.

d) By all possible diligence and frugality, that the gospel be not blamed.

e) By running with patience the race which is set before them, denying themselves, and taking up their cross daily; submitting to bear the reproach of Christ, to be as the filth and offscouring of the world; and looking that men should say all manner of evil of them *falsely*, for the Lord's sake.

It is expected of all who desire to continue in these societies that they should continue to evidence their desire of salvation.

THIRDLY: By attending upon all the ordinances of God; such are:

a) The public worship of God.

b) The ministry of the Word, either read or expounded.

c) The Supper of the Lord.

d) Family and private prayer.

e) Searching the Scriptures.

f) Fasting or abstinence.

These are the General Rules of our societies; all of which we are taught of God to observe, even in his written Word, which is the only rule, and the sufficient rule, both of our faith and practice. And all these we know his Spirit writes on truly awakened hearts. If there be any among us who observe them not, who habitually break any of them, let it be known unto them who watch over that soul as they who must give an account. We will admonish him of the error of his ways. We will bear with him for a season. But then, if he repent not, he hath no more place among us. We have delivered our own souls. —*John Wesley, Charles Wesley May 1, 1743*

APPENDIX B

Charles Wesley's "A Prayer for Those Who Are Convinced of Sin"[17]

O most compassionate High Priest
Full of all grace we know thou art
Faith puts its hands upon thy breast,
And feels beneath thy panting heart.

Thy panting heart for sinners bleeds;
Thy mercies and compassions move;
The groaning Spirit intercedes,
And yearn the bowels of thy love.

Hear then the pleading Spirit's prayer
(The Spirit's will to thee is known)
For all who now thy sufferings share,
And still for full redemption groan.

Poor tempted souls, with tempests tossed,
And strangers to a moment's peace,
Disconsolate, afflicted, lost—
Lost in the howling wilderness.

Torn with an endless war within,
Vexed with the flesh and spirit's strife,
And struggling in the toils of sin,
And agonizing into life.

O let the pris'ners' mournful cries
As incense in thy sight appear,
Their humble wailings pierce the skies,
If haply they may feel thee near!

The captive exiles make their moans,
From sin impatient to be free;
Call home, call home thy banished ones!
Lead captive their captivity!

Show them the blood that bought their peace,
The anchor of their steadfast hope,
And bid their guilty terrors cease,
And bring the ransomed pris'ners up.

Out of the deep regard their cries,
The fallen raise, the mourners cheer;
The Sun of righteousness, arise,
And scatter all their doubt and fear!

Pity the day of feeble things;
O gather ev'ry halting soul;
And drop salvation from thy wings,
And make the contrite sinner whole.

Stand by them in the fiery hour,
Their feebleness of mind defend.
And in their weakness show thy power,
And make them patient to the end.

O satisfy their soul in drought;
Give them thy saving health to see,
And let thy mercy find them out;
And let thy mercy reach to me.

Hast thou the work of grace begun,
And brought them to the birth in vain?
O let thy children see the son!
Let all their souls be born again!

Relieve the souls whose cross we bear,
for whom thy suffering members mourn,
Answer our faith's effectual prayer,
Bid ev'ry struggling child be born

Hark how thy turtle dove complains,
And see we weep for Zion's woe!
Pity thy suffering people's pain;
Avenge us of our inbred foe.

Whom thou hast bound, O Lord, expel,
And take his armour all away;
The man of sin, the child of hell,
The devil in our nature slay.

Him and his works at once destroy,
The *being* of all sin release.
And turn our mourning into joy,
And clothe us with robes of praise.

Then when our sufferings all are past.
O let us pure and perfect be,
And gain our calling's prize at last,
Forever sanctified in thee.

ENDNOTES

1. Marjorie Thompson, *Soul Feast: An Introduction to the Christian Spiritual Life* (Louisville, KY: Westminster/John Knox Press, 1995), 138.

2. See Para. 103 in *2008 edition of The Book of Discipline of the United Methodist Church*.

3. See "General Rules of the United Societies" in *The Works of John Wesley* edited by Rupert E. Davies Vol. 9 *The Methodist Societies: History, Nature and Design* (Nashville, TN: Abingdon Press, 1989), 69.

4. Ibid., 69-70.

5. Ibid., 70.

6. I am borrowing this phrase from Fr. James Heft, the former Provost of Dayton University, who has spoken often of the kind of disciplined company that is necessary to give and receive hospitality in Catholic higher education as being "an open circle." See his essay "The Open Circle: The Culture of the Catholic University" in *Australian E-Journal in Theology* (February 2004) Issue 2 ISSN 1448-632.

7. I am indebted to Rev. Dr. Andrew Kinsey, Senior Pastor of Grace United Methodist Church in Franklin, Indiana for calling this matter to my attention in his unpublished paper, "Radical Orthodoxy As Remedy?"

8. Scott Jones, *John Wesley's Conception and Use of Scripture* (Nashville, TN: Kingswood Books, 1995), 124.

9. Vicki Tolar Burton, *Spiritual Literacy* in John Wesley's *Methodism: Reading, Writing, and Speaking to Believe* (Waco, TX: Baylor University Press, 2008).

10. Lester Ruth, *Early Methodist Life and Spirituality: A Reader* (Nashville, TN: Kingswood Books, 2005), 226.

11. Ibid., 225.

12. Ibid.

13. Richard P. Heitzenrater, *John Wesley and the People Called Methodists* (Nashville, TN: Abingdon Press, 1995), 47. "Wesley's Covenant Service," *The United Methodist Book of Worship*, (Nashville, TN: The United Methodist Publishing House, 1992) No. 291.

14. See "General Rules of the United Societies" in *The Works of John Wesley* edited, Vol. 9, p. 73.

15. Here, I am grateful to the insights of James William McClendon for calling my attention to John Howard Yoder's Stone Lectures at Princeton Theological Seminary where Yoder commented so provocatively on the text of Acts 27:1-44. See McClendon's *Systematic Theology: Vol. 3 Witness* (Nashville, TN: Abingdon, 2001), 15-16.

16. *The Upper Room Worshipbook: Music and Liturgies for Spiritual Formation* (Nashville, TN: Upper Room Books, 1982), 113.

17. "A Prayer for Those Convinced of Sin," in *The Works of John Wesley*, Vol.9, 73-75. See also note #36 on p. 73, which provides the following information: *This composition* by Charles Wesley was published in his Hymns and Sacred Poems (Bristol, Farley, 1749), II, 89-91. The poem was included in all English editions of the General Rules except the 4th, 1744 (which contained the Band Rules), and that in Wesley's Works.

Wesleyan ConneXion Project

*A clergy leadership formation program of the
Indiana Conference of the United Methodist Church*

Printed in Great Britain
by Amazon